ATLAS OF MICRONESIA

SECOND EDITION

Bruce G. Karolle

Bess Press
P.O. Box 22388
Honolulu, Hawaii 96823

CONTRIBUTORS

Contributing Authors	*Section*
Richard D. Krizman, Natural Sciences, UOG	Climate and Weather; Vegetation
Rosalind Hunter-Anderson, formerly WERI, UOG	Prehistory
Dirk Anthony Ballendorf, MARC, UOG	Foreign Rule: 1668-1945
Reilly Ridgell, Guam Community College	Geographic Names
Velma A. Sablan, Assistant Professor, UOG	Distance Education

Director of Cartography: Bruce G. Karolle

Cover art: Christine Joy Pratt

Cover design: Paula Newcomb

Graphic Artists: Conrado Redila, Richard D. Krizman, Pramila Sullivan, and Bruce G. Karolle

Editorial Assistance: Richard Ypenberg, Phyllis Koontz, Frank P. King, and Bruce G. Karolle

Photographs: MARC Photo Collection, Richard Krizman, and Bruce G. Karolle

First edition credits:
University of Guam Student Consultants: Sabino Sauchomal, Satawal, Yap; Loreda Mwianur, Puluwat, Truk; Grace Joseph, Truk; Simeon Refilong, Truk; Penito S. Timothy, Truk; Ketsen Fritz Haregaichig, Truk; Vancent Moses, Truk; Edward Robert, Kosrae; Wilton Mackwelung, Kosrae; Saberiano Barnabas, Pohnpei; Sister Mary Benedict, Rota.

SPECIAL ACKNOWLEDGMENTS FOR MANUSCRIPT READING: Lee S. Motteler, Bishop Museum, Honolulu; Don and Edith Worsencroft, Honomu, Hawaii; Fran Hezel, Chuuk (Truk); UOG Professors: Yigal Zan, Marvin Montvel-Cohen, and Douglas R. Smith, Guam.

A SPECIAL ACKNOWLEDGMENT FOR FUNDING: A support grant from the School of the Pacific Islands, Inc., Thousand Oaks, California.

Library of Congress Catalog Card Number: 93-71647

Karolle, Bruce G.
    Atlas of Micronesia, 2nd ed.
    Honolulu, Hawaii: The Bess Press, Inc.
    128 pages

ISBN: 1-880188-50-3

TABLE OF CONTENTS

List of FIGURES

List of TABLES

List of PHOTOGRAPHS

FOREWORD

This atlas is intended as a basic reference for libraries, schools, government agencies, and the general reader. The second edition is an expansion of the first edition; in addition to several new topical coverages, i.e., island vegetation, early exploration, place-name examination, economic growth of tourism, and distance education, there are also statistical and name updates in this edition.

This volume covers the portion of the western Pacific Ocean called Micronesia. Emphasis is placed on the archipelagic areas of the Mariana, Caroline, and Marshall Islands, with special regard for the major characteristics of the region's natural, man-made, and human resources. A thematic map presentation includes population distributions, fish and marine resources, political and economic boundaries, climate and rainfall, and historical and cultural developments. The book comprises maps, graphs, photographs, drawings, and text designed to reveal the complexity of the area.

Introductory text overviews each of the sections that deal with the significant aspects of Micronesia's culture, economy, history, and natural environment. Also, explanatory textual material accompanies all individual maps and data tables.

This reference atlas is composed of three sections: Part 1. **General**, which attempts to demonstrate Micronesia's regional ties with Southeast and East Asia, as well as show its trans-Pacific connections; Part 2. **Micronesia**, which focuses on several important areal presentations and a single topical article (canoe navigation), and includes an easy-to-read gazetteer listing the main islands; and Part 3. **Individual Islands and Atolls**, which selects key insular areas for large-scale emphases of individual physical and human geographic characteristics.

The three sections provide the reader with an integrated landscape view of the region. Each section emphasizes a regional perspective with regard for topical themes. Every attempt has been made to clarify complex information or terminology and geographic concepts for the non-specialist reader. The graphic material has been designed to be as self-explanatory as possible.

PART 1 - GENERAL

Introduction

The designation "Micronesia," as used throughout this atlas, refers to a geographic area encompassing an enormous expanse of the tropical western Pacific Ocean. Defined and delimited as an areal unit, or a portion of the earth's surface, it comprises a recognized region of the world and has been in use on maps for over 160 years.

As the first two maps indicate in Figures 1 and 2 (pages 2 and 3), land makes up a mere 1,045.3 square miles (2,707.2 km²) of this oceanic region whose area is well in excess of three million square miles (>7 million km²). Micronesia is one of the three major ethno-geographical regions, or designations, of the Pacific World, or Oceania, the other two being Polynesia and Melanesia.

The Region

The name Micronesia, derived from the Greek words *mikros* (small) and *nesos* (island), was first used in 1831 by Domeny de Rienzi in a submission to the *Société de Géographie de Paris*. There are several island groups and newly established island states within the region: the Federated States of Micronesia, the Republic of the Marshall Islands (both FSM and RMI became member states of the UN on 1 OCT 91), the Republic of Belau, the Commonwealth of the Northern Mariana Islands - all of which constituted the former Trust Territory of the Pacific Islands (TTPI) - Guam, Nauru, and the Gilbert Islands, including Banaba (formerly Ocean Island) in the Republic of Kiribati. Table 1 (page 4) indicates the number and area of these individual islands, island groups, and entities.

The Caroline Islands, a vast east-west archipelago, includes five districts of the former Trust Territory: Kosrae, Pohnpei, Truk, Yap, and Palau. Of these, the first four have constituted themselves as states of a new political entity called the Federated States of Micronesia (FSM). The entire archipelago comprises 957 islands, islets, and reefs with a total land area of 461.441 square miles (1,195.1 km²).

The Marshall Islands numbers 1,225 islands, islets, and reefs with a total land area of 69.840 square miles (180.87 km²).

The Commonwealth of the Northern Mariana Islands (CNMI) numbers 20 islands, islets, and reefs with a total land area of 184.508 square miles (477.85 km²).

Guam, the southernmost island of the Mariana archipelago, and its associated reef complexes, is approximately 214 square miles (554.2 km²) in area. It has been an unincorporated territory of the United States since 1898, and thus has a different political status from the other islands of Micronesia. Guam and the islands of the former Trust Territory together - referred to here as American Micronesia - account for 929.789 square miles (2,408.1 km²) which is approximately eighty-nine percent of the total land area of Micronesia.

The remaining Micronesian islands are the Gilbert Islands (Republic of Kiribati), with a land area of 104.92 square miles (271.7 km²); Banaba (Ocean Island), also a part of Kiribati, with 2.4 square miles (6.7 km²); and the Republic of Nauru (formerly administered by Australia under a League of Nations mandate, and subsequently under a United Nations trusteeship), with a land area of 8.2 square miles (21.2 km²).

Micronesian Geographic Distances

The general boundaries of the geographic region of Micronesia are shown in Figures 1 and 2. The maps outline an 11-sided polygon located in the western Pacific Ocean. The extremes of latitude cover approximately 23 degrees. The northern-most land point in Micronesia is on the island of Farallon de Pajaros in the Mariana Islands at 20.33 degrees north latitude; the southernmost point is in the Gilbert Islands, Kiribati, on Arorae at 2.39 degrees south latitude. The maximum north to south distance is thus 1,387.2 nautical miles, or 1,595.28 statute miles.

The east-west distances are even greater, covering over 45 degrees of longitude. The distance between the small island of Tobi, in Palau, within a few hundred miles of Indonesia and the Philippines, at 131.10 degrees east longitude, and the easternmost atoll of Arorae, Kiribati, at 176.54 degrees east longitude, is approximately 2,726 nautical miles (3,135 statute miles), or about the same as the distance across the United States from coast to coast.

The great distances separating the various islands and political entities within Micronesia play a determining role in transportation difficulties in the region. As an example, the airport-to-airport distances - in the Federated States of Micronesia - between the state capitals, or

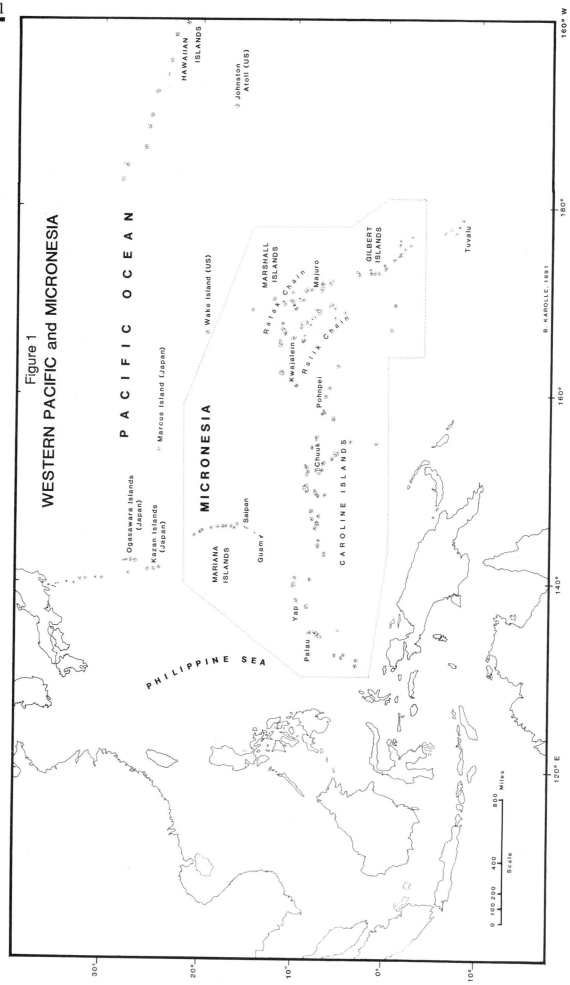

Figure 1
WESTERN PACIFIC and MICRONESIA

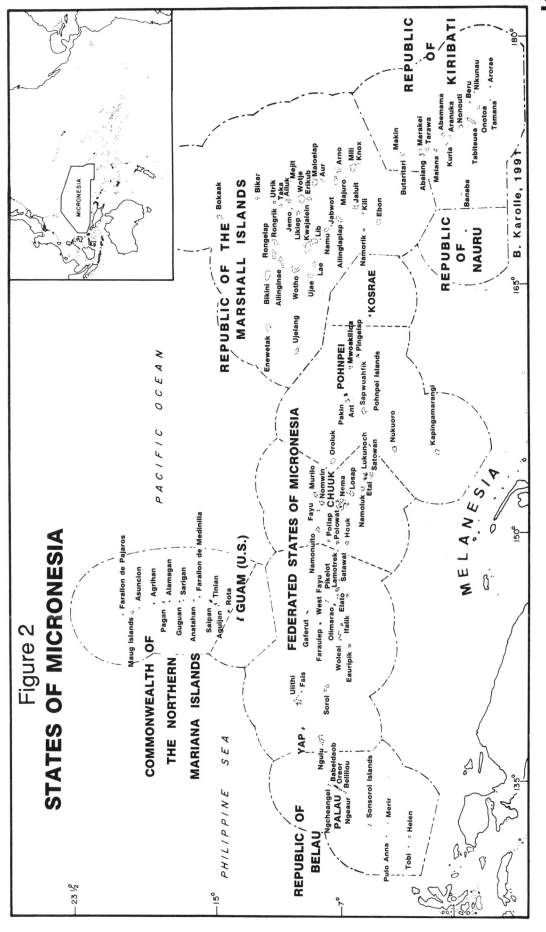

Figure 2
STATES OF MICRONESIA

Table 1. Insular Areas of Micronesia

NAME	NUMBER OF ISLANDS (Total # of individual islets/reefs)	SIZE IN SQUARE MILES	SIZE BY GROUP AND POLITICAL TERRITORY
Caroline Islands (west to east)			
Palau Islands (Republic of Belau)	350	190.655	190.655
Yap Islands	149	45.925	
Truk Islands	290	49.181	
Pohnpei	163	133.364	
Kosrae	5	42.316	
(Federated States of Micronesia)		270.786	270.786
Subtotals:	957	461.441	461.441
Marshall Islands (Republic of the Marshall Islands)	1,225	69.840	69.840
Northern Mariana Islands (U.S. Commonwealth of the Northern Mariana Islands)	20	184.508	184.508
		TOTAL: (Former TTPI)	715.789
Guam (U.S. Territory)	1	214.000	214.000
		TOTAL: American Micronesia	929.789
Nauru (Republic of Nauru)	1	8.200	8.200
Gilbert Islands	168	104.919	8.200
Banaba (Ocean) (Republic of Kiribati)	1	2.417	107.336
		TOTAL: Dry-land area of Micronesia	1,045.325

Sources: Bryan, 1971.
Tarawa Teacher's College, 1976.
Karolle, 1981.

district centers as they used to be called, are listed below:

Island-to-Island	Nautical miles
Pohnpei - Kosrae	320
Truk (Moen) - Pohnpei	380
Yap - Pohnpei	1,200
Yap - Kosrae	1,500

These data illustrate the problem of geographic fragmentation throughout the region. This may be seen in the following list of distances from Guam, which is the communication and transportation hub of American Micronesia:

Island-to-Island	Nautical miles (airport-to-airport, total accrued distance)
Guam - Truk	551
Guam - Yap	466
Guam - Palau	711
Guam - Truk - Pohnpei - Majuro	1,709

On a larger view, Figure 3 (page 6) illustrates approximate distances from Guam in a series of expanding concentric circles..

The Physical Geography of Micronesia

Within Micronesia, a geologic or structural boundary separates the region into two major physiographic provinces. These consist of the Pacific Basin or Plate (characterized as the largest physical earth region and the largest of the three physiographic provinces of the Pacific realm) and the Western Margins, including the Philippine Plate. (See Figure 4, page 7.) The third major physical province of the Pacific realm is the Pacific Rim, which is located in the coastal North Pacific Ocean of Alaska extending down the coastal mountains and valleys of North America and reaching southern California and the adjacent plate boundaries of the eastern Pacific Ocean in Middle and South America.

The focus of this physical boundary in Micronesia is known as the "andesite line," which separates the Pacific Basin from the Philippine Plate, and identifies those particular Micronesian islands that form the eastern edge of the Philippine Plate. These curved and arcing island groups are

called collectively the Rimlands (refer to Figures 5 and 10, pages 8 and 22), and they consist of the main islands of Palau, Yap, and the Mariana Islands. Toward the convex sides of the Rimlands, to the east, are the deep trenches of the Pacific Basin.

If we were to diagram a surface or topographic profile of the Philippine Sea floor passing through the Mariana Islands into the Pacific Ocean, then a generalized surface configuration would look something like Figure 5. In other words, this significant physiographic delimitation in Micronesia is a boundary between the Pacific Basin floor and the island structures (volcanic mountains) of the Philippine Sea. The Palau Islands, Yap Islands (excluding Ulithi and the other outer islands and atolls of Yap State), Guam and the other Marianas, Kazan (formerly the Volcano Islands), the Ogasawara (formerly the Bonin Islands), and the Izu Shichito Islands extending to Honshu, Japan, constitute a section of the andesite line which divides the deeper Pacific from the partially submerged continental areas on its western margins.

Ocean Floors and Subduction

It has long been known that the ocean floor is composed of basins interrupted by mountains that rise to the ocean surface, forming islands. Often these mountain-top islands are isolated features, but again and again they form great chains of islands that extend over hundreds of miles. Within Micronesia, there exist several of these island chains, which have been identified as unified archipelagoes.

Scientists have determined that the earth's outer covering, known as the crust of the earth, is made up of both continents and ocean floors that together form a rather rigid outer shell of the earth called the lithosphere. Figure 6 (page 8) shows the depth of the earth's crust, which consists of the lithosphere (divided into various earth surface plates) atop the partially molten rock of the mantle or asthenosphere.

It is now understood that the heat of the subcrustal earth passes as convection currents into the asthenosphere. These currents of energy cause movement in the lithosphere or in the various ocean plates and into the continents as well.

The ocean floor movements of rising and spreading have been identified as the subject of plate tectonics, replacing the older theory of

Figure 3. Map Distances

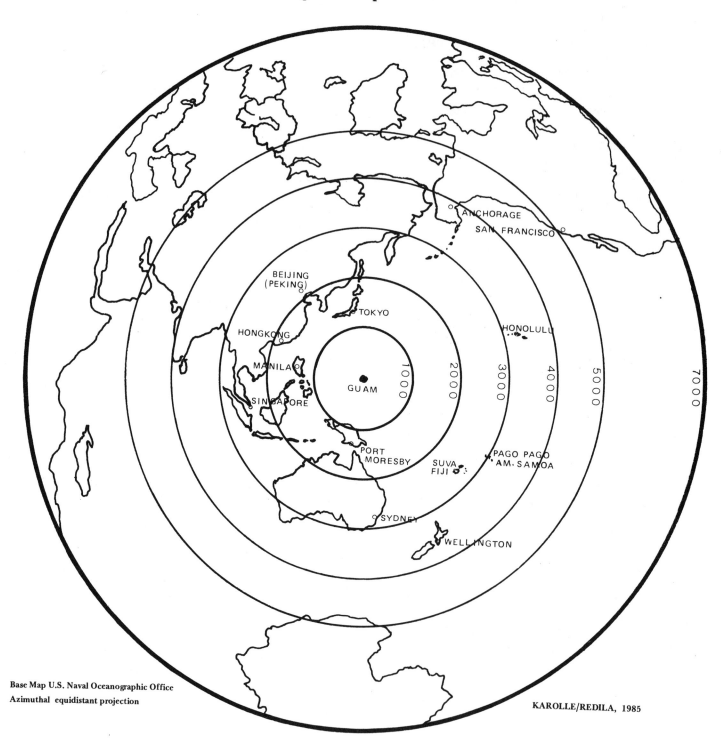

Base Map U.S. Naval Oceanographic Office
Azimuthal equidistant projection

KAROLLE/REDILA, 1985

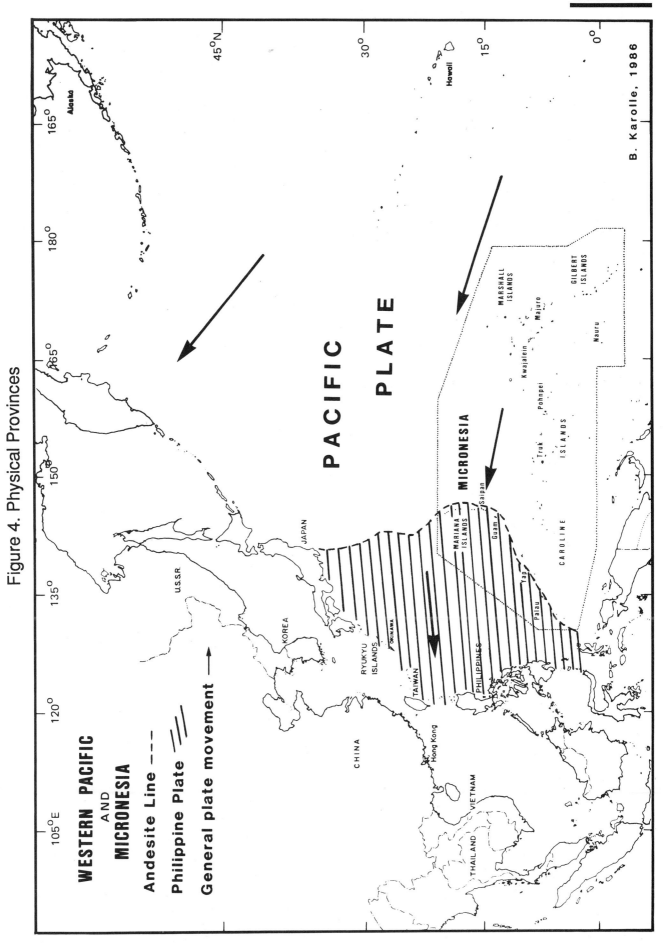

Figure 4. Physical Provinces

B. Karolle, 1986

WESTERN PACIFIC
AND
MICRONESIA

Andesite Line ———

Philippine Plate ///

General plate movement ——→

PACIFIC PLATE

MICRONESIA

Alaska

U.S.S.R.

JAPAN

KOREA

CHINA

Hong Kong

VIETNAM

THAILAND

RYUKYU ISLANDS

OKINAWA

TAIWAN

PHILIPPINES

Palau

Yap

Guam

Saipan

MARIANA ISLANDS

CAROLINE ISLANDS

Truk

Pohnpei

Kwajalein

Majuro

MARSHALL ISLANDS

Nauru

GILBERT ISLANDS

Hawaii

105°E 120° 135° 150° 165° 180° 165° 45°N 30° 15° 0°

Figure 5. Profile of the Marianas and the Rimlands

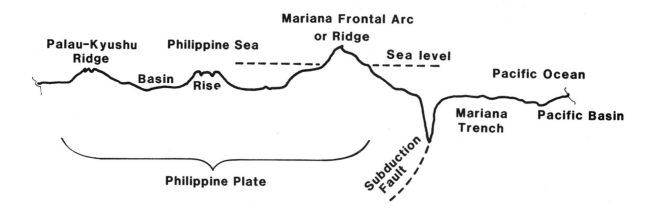

(East-west cross-section not to scale)

B. Karolle, 1989

Figure 6. Earth Structure: both continental and oceanic crusts atop the lithosphere

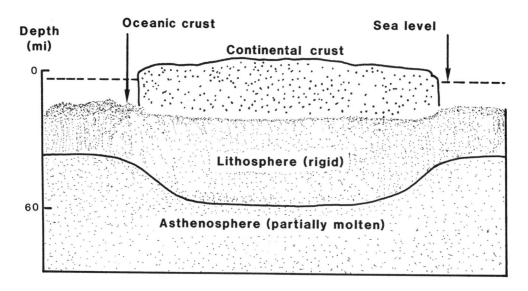

(after Oliver, 1979)

continental drift, and can be illustrated as shown in Figure 7, below. The Pacific Plate in the far eastern Pacific Ocean area experiences sea-floor spreading and upwelling of magma or mountain building, while in the western Pacific and Micronesia the spreading or dragging action becomes known as subduction. Where the convection currents descend in the lithosphere, the ocean floor of the Mariana Trench is dragged downward into the asthenosphere. Along this fault zone, where the subduction takes place, many earthquakes occur.

Earthquakes

Earthquakes occur regularly in specific areas of Micronesia. To understand how often and why they occur requires us to identify the geographical particulars of the area. Within the region, a physical ocean floor boundary exists that we have identified as the subduction boundary zone and the Micronesian island chains of the Rimlands.

First of all, this physical boundary includes Guam and the whole Marianas archipelago extending in a curved line from the distant Palau Islands, some 800 miles southwest of Guam, and northward to Japan, about 1,500 miles to the northeast. Actually, this western Pacific boundary - often referred to as part of the "Rim of Fire" surrounding the Pacific Ocean - divides the region of Micronesia. This physiographic boundary separates the deeper Pacific from the submerged continental margins of the Philippine Sea. What we have then is the Pacific Basin on the eastern side

Figure 7. Plate Tectonics: (a) sea floor movement

(b) subduction of Pacific plate

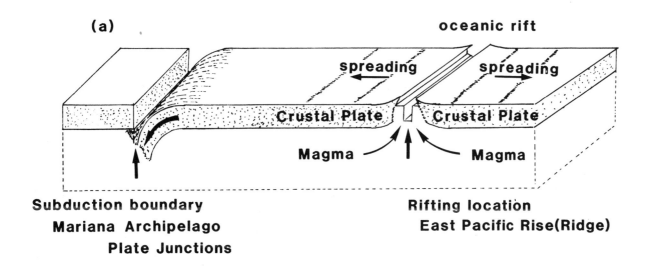

(a)

oceanic rift

spreading   spreading

Crustal Plate   Crustal Plate

Magma   Magma

Subduction boundary
Mariana Archipelago
Plate Junctions

Rifting location
East Pacific Rise(Ridge)

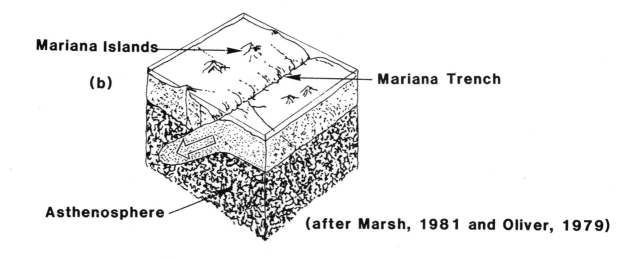

Mariana Islands

(b)

Mariana Trench

Asthenosphere

(after Marsh, 1981 and Oliver, 1979)

of Guam, where the Pacific Basin meets the Mariana Trench adjacent to the Mariana archipelago, concavely facing the Asian continent and the Philippine Islands some 1,500 miles to the west. (See Figures 4 and 5.)

The subject of earthquakes necessarily overlaps into the physical sciences of natural history and geological studies. The topical studies of continental drift, plate tectonics, and volcanism provide an understanding of why the Rimland islands have so many shakes and quakes.

The earth's crust is anything but permanent and stable. It undergoes constant change ranging from imperceptible isostatic adjustment to violent deformation during earthquakes and volcanic outbursts. There are areas, however, where the crust is less stable than it is elsewhere. The earth's most earthquake-prone belts surround the Pacific Ocean and cross Eurasia along the Alps and the Himalayas. The mid-ocean ridges can also be discerned as belts of frequent earthquakes. The shield areas of the continents, such as in Scandinavia and Finland, on the other hand, are much less affected.

Earthquakes originate in Micronesia along the subduction zone and occur within three miles of the ocean floor. Fortunately for the Rimland islands, the bottom of the trenches in the Pacific floor areas lies about six miles beneath the point of origin of the earthquake. The location directly above this focus, at the surface of the crust, is the epicenter. The Philippine Plate area on the map shows the location of volcanoes and the associated epicenters. (See Figures 4 and 7.)

An earthquake results from the sudden movement of rock that has been subjected to prolonged stress. When the two lithospheric plates collide with the Pacific Plate, moving downward and underneath the Philippine Plate, stresses are set up that cause certain rock to fracture. Such fractures in the lithosphere are called faults. Some, such as the San Andreas Fault in California, are well known as the source of repeated earthquakes.

The northern volcano on Pagan island, located in the Northern Marianas, erupted in 1981. The earthquake registered 4.5 on the Richter scale and destroyed the single village on that isolated island. The fifty-three villagers evacuated have relocated in other islands of the Northern Marianas and apparently have no intention of returning to live in Pagan on a permanent basis.

In recent years, earthquakes have caused considerable damage on Guam. They occurred in 1970 (6.0), 1975 (6.25), and 1978 (5.5) - the Richter magnitudes are in parentheses. The November 27, 1975, earthquake caused an estimated $500,000 in damage to the island, while the January 27, 1978, occurrence saw $250,000 in government funds released to the local victims for structural - mainly building - repairs.

Earthquakes are monitored by Guam observatories at Northwest Field (Potts Junction) and Mt. Santa Rosa in Yigo. The observatories are operated by the U.S. Geological Survey; these facilities are part of a world-wide network of reporting stations measuring seismic activities.

Volcanic Islands and Atolls

The islands of Micronesia may be divided into two major physiographic types: the high volcanic islands and the low coral atolls. Several other categories exist, but these basic distinctions describe and correspond to "high-island" and "low-island" culture types.

The high-island cultures developed on the better-watered volcanic islands, while the low-island cultures evolved on the sometimes drought-stricken coral atolls. Traditionally, agriculture and fishing were the bases of subsistence on all these islands. A certain complementarity between the agriculture-based island economies and those based on fishing continues to exist, as the low-coral-island people still are skilled canoe sailors and fishermen.

The inhabitants of the high and low islands and their cultures have become altered by Western contact in recent times. Often in this process, they have forsaken subsistence farming and fishing for government employment and and welfare programs.

The Atoll Environments

Atolls are the most numerous and distinctive form of coral (calcareous) reef in Micronesia. (See Figure 8, page 11.) There are seventy-two of them widespread throughout the Caroline, Marshall, and Gilbert Islands. The Gilbert archipelago consists of atolls or "almost" atolls; there are sixteen of them in that part of Kiribati. Eighty percent of the total number of islands in the Marshalls are atolls, and slightly more than half of the Carolines also are of this type. (See Figure 12, page ??.)

Atolls are reefs of organic limestone grown or built on top of slightly submerged volcanic

Figure 8. Topographic Profile of an Atoll

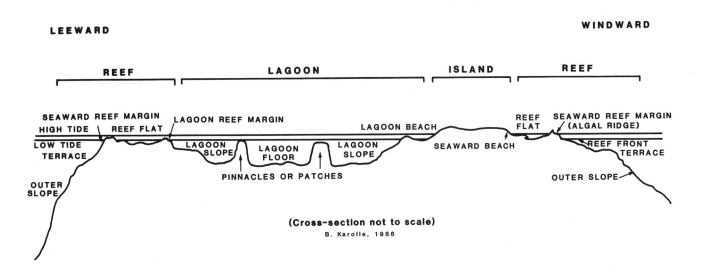

LEEWARD   WINDWARD

(Cross-section not to scale)
B. Karolle, 1986

Figure 9. Atoll Profiles

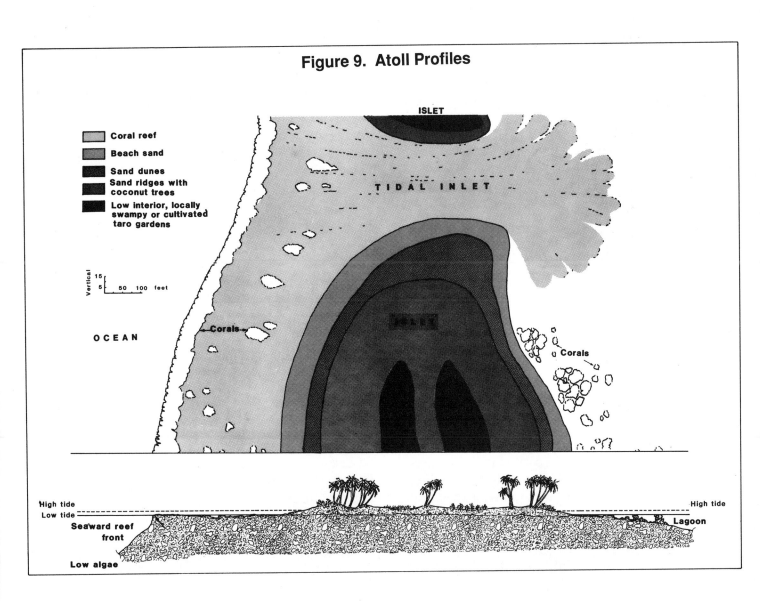

mountains. They are partly, intermittently, or continuously covered by water. An atoll is thus a limestone cap - commonly bowl-shaped at the surface with a ringlike ridge or reef enclosing a body of water or lagoon - in turn surrounded by the open sea. As land features, atolls are discontinuous and consist mainly of low, sandy islets which result from the accumulation of limestone debris (either loose or consolidated) and occasional remnants of former high reef surfaces. The major islets of an atoll complex are usually not more than ten feet above high-tide level, except for storm-built rubble ridges and wind-deposited dunes, which rise a few feet higher.

The primary components of an atoll (Figures 8 and 9, page 11) are the outer slope, reef front, seaward reef margin, reef flat, beach, islets, lagoon reef margin, lagoon slope, and lagoon floor. Islets are most frequent on the eastern, or windward, sectors of the reef rim. Almost three-quarters of all atolls have islets on less than one-half of their circumference. The largest and widest islets coincide with wide portions of the reef where sharp outward bends occur. Reef widths tend to be greater in the general direction of prevailing winds, currents, and waves. Deep passes through reef rims, navigable by oceangoing vessels, occur most frequently on the leeward or sheltered sides of atolls where reef growth is less vigorous or is inhibited.

Waves commonly break on the seaward reef margin, and water flows from the sea to the lagoon and back to the sea over the reef flat or through gaps in it. The flow may be in or out with the tides, or in over the windward and out over the leeward sides.

The Plant Life of Micronesia

In the distant past the islands of Micronesia were lifeless formations of rock or coral debris. All of the vegetation which we now call indigenous, or native, arrived from elsewhere by four methods.

Of these the most effective was transportation of seeds by birds and other flying animals. Small, sticky, or barbed seeds were carried in the feathers, on the legs and feet, or in mud clinging to toes or claws. Seeds resistant to digestion were carried in the digestive tract. Wide-ranging migratory and marine birds are most likely to have been involved in this dispersal process.

A second method of airborne distribution was on the wind, which carried the minute seeds of orchids and the minuscule spores of ferns over great distances. Seeds slightly heavier than these, but equipped with plumes or fluff or ballooned on spider silk, also could have been borne by the wind over wide expanses of ocean.

Floating and rafting are two methods of transportation by water. In the first, the seeds, or seed-bearing fruits, need to be buoyant and resistant to prolonged immersion in sea water. Successful migration then depended on whether the seeds eventually reached a hospitable shore where germination, establishment, and colonization could take place.

Seeds and small plants also may be rafted over considerable distances on anything from mere sticks to masses of tangled trees. Whether such seeds or plants are then able to establish themselves in a new location, is, again, entirely a matter of chance arrival in a favorable environment.

The geographic origins of the coastal flora of Micronesia cannot be determined. Most of these species are found in broad areas of the Indo-Pacific region. Others occur as far afield as East Africa and a few flourish in tropical zones throughout the world. In contrast, the plants of the interiors of the larger and higher islands have narrower distribution and their geographical origins can be more closely determined. Most have affinities with the flora of the Indo-Malaysian region, other Pacific tropical islands, and the tropical reaches of the Old World. The indigenous flora of the island interiors often include numerous endemic - locally evolved - species. Subsequent to arrival, these species adapted and specialized to form new species.

As a result of the small size and relatively limited ecological diversity of most Micronesian islands, their numbers of plant species is generally small. Another factor influencing numbers is distance from sources of plant migration, the greater the distance, the smaller the number of species.

Besides the indigenous or native flora of Micronesia, a relatively large number of species have been introduced by man following the first European (Ferdinand Magellan) contact in 1521. Some of these introductions were by accident, but others were brought to the islands intentionally. Many of the chance arrivals are now common herbaceous weeds. Intentionally introduced plants, in the main, are of the "useful" ones, that is to say, plants perceived as having economic value. Besides food plants, numerous other species were introduced for all sorts of purposes, from dye production to medicinal uses and ornamentation.

Some of the introduced species have become naturalized, or have "gone wild," and are now able to reproduce and maintain themselves without human assistance. In some cases, it is by no means obvious whether such a species is introduced or indigenous.

Other introduced species clearly could never survive without human care. These are often the house, yard, and farm plants.

It has been established that there are 1,228 species of indigenous higher plants in Micronesia, 566, or 46 percent of which, are endemic. All of the endemic plants, with one or two exceptions, are found in the Caroline and Mariana Islands. (See Table 2, page 14.)

Another 1,015 species are classified as introduced by man; in other words, 45 percent of all species were brought from elsewhere. (See Table 3, page 15.)

The vegetation of the inhabited areas of Micronesia is highly disturbed, manipulated, and utilized. The interiors of the inhabited low islands have been extensively altered through coconut and breadfruit cultivation and by taro pits. Coastal vegetation, by contrast, has usually been left relatively undisturbed.

The coastal vegetation of high and low islands is broadly similar. (See Photo 1, page 16.) Major components of the coastal flora include *Messerschmidia* (=*Tournifortia*), *Scaevola*, *Pemphis*, *Guettarda*, *Hernandia*, *Terminalia*, *Suriana*, and *Barringtonia asiatica*. Immediately beyond the shoreline in the coastal lowlands, where most of the human population lives, the environment is highly managed. "Useful" plants predominate here and most other vegetation has been eliminated. The centers of most high islands are mountainous, and the vegetation of these highlands remains comparatively undisturbed. The interiors of islands like Kosrae and Pohnpei are almost impenetrable as trails become unused, overgrown, and forgotten.

Attempts to raise crops in Micronesia have always encountered problems, with poor soils being the major obstacle. In the tropics, nutrients are held within the vegetation, and as individual plants die and decay those nutrients are quickly recycled. Nutrients do not accumulate in the soil, because they are leached away by heavy rainfall. Once vegetation is removed, few nutrients remain to support agriculture.

Perennial insect pests and plant diseases are other problems. Where in temperate zones low winter temperatures deter insects and diseases, equable tropical climates encourage them. An added menace is tropical downpours, which often wash out or drown plants. Conversely, even a few weeks without rain can desiccate the porous soils. Finally, tropical storms and typhoons not uncommonly destroy any agricultural endeavor.

In eastern Micronesia, the fifty or so atolls and other low coral islands of the Marshall and Gilbert Islands are distributed north to south, with the smallest islands in the far north. The islands increase in size toward the south from around two square miles to about eight. Though varying in size, all the islands are physiographically similar.

As one traverses the island chain from north to south, the relationship between the lateral layering of precipitation and the increasing and decreasing prevalence of plant species becomes obvious. The chain has been divided into nine vegetation zones. In the northernmost islands, Zone 1, we first encounter low, open scrub forest, with only a dozen or two indigenous species, so arid that coconut trees do not thrive. Zone 2, to the south, is slightly wetter and coconut trees normally are able to develop. Large *Pisonia* trees may form continuous forest here. In Zone 3, which includes Enewetak (Eniwetok) atoll, coconut trees have been planted and forests contain *Cordia* and *Pemphis*. Kwajalein atoll is in Zone 4. It has extensive coconut plantations, many breadfruit trees, and forests of *Neisosperma* (*Ochrosia*). Majuro atoll is situated in Zone 5. Coconut and breadfruit trees grow very tall here and their productivity is high. The luxuriant vegetation includes thick undergrowth.

Zone 6, the southernmost in the Marshalls, receives the most rain. Vegetation is luxuriant and the largest number of species, well in excess of 100, is found here. There also is some mangrove forest in this zone. Farther southward into the Gilberts, rainfall diminishes, with the vegetation becoming less complex. Consequently, Zone 7 is comparable to Zone 5. Zone 8, including Tarawa atoll, may be likened to Zone 4, characterized by open undergrowth. Finally, the southernmost belt, Zone 9, just south of the equator, corresponds to Zone 3.

Table 2. Numbers of endemic higher plant species present in Micronesian Island groups.

==

PLANT CATEGORY	ISLAND GROUPS					
	MARIANA	CAROLINE	BOTH*	MARSHALL	GILBERT	TOTAL
Ferns	3 (10%)**	26 (84%)	2 (6%)	0	0	3 1 (5%)***
Gymno-sperms	0	0	0	0	0	0
Monocots	19 (11%)	135 (81%)	11 (7%)	1 (0.6%)	0	166 (29%)
Dicots	78 (21%)	267 (72%)	4 (7%)	0	0	369 (65%)
TOTAL	100 (18%)	428 (76%)	37 (7%)	1 (0.2%) :	0	566

==

SOURCES:

F. R. Fosberg, M.-H. Sachet, and R. Oliver, 1979, 1982, and 1987.

 * Endemic to both the Mariana and Caroline Islands.
 ** Island percentages are percents of totals at right (e.g., 3/31 = 10%).
 *** Percentages at right are percents of overall total (e.g., 31/566 = 5%).

The Caroline Islands, a scattering of both low and high islands, stretch over some 2,000 miles of ocean. They are located in the latitude of maximum rainfall, which means a generally evenly spaced 150 to 200 inches per annum. Vegetation on the low islands is similar to that of the southern Marshalls, with relatively few species, a lack of endemic plants, and a preponderance of widely distributed strand flora.

On Pohnpei, the major island of the eastern Carolines, four broad vegetation communities are recognized: mangrove forest, strand vegetation, secondary growth of the lowlands, and rain forest, and secondary growth of uplands. The mangrove forests (*Rhizophora*, *Bruguiera*, and *Sonneratia*) are extensive, as is the case on other high islands in the Carolines. As mangrove forests encircle the island,

except in cleared areas (see Photo 2, page 16), the strand vegetation (see Photo 1, page 16) is meager. Due to centuries of human activity, a zone of secondary lowland vegetation, consisting mainly of cultivated and naturalized plants, has taken the place of the original vegetation. It extends inland to an elevation of about 800 feet. The zone includes grasslands which once may have been cultivated areas.

The uplands, 100 to 1,000 feet, are dominated by tall trees of the species *Campnosperma* (family *Anacardiaceae*). (See Photo 3, page 17.) Between 360 to 2,200 feet, a tall endemic palm, *Exorrliza* (*Climostigma*), forms dense forests. From 2,000 feet to summits at about 2,500 feet are tree ferns, *Cyathea ponapeana*, and an endemic pandanus, *P. patina*. Above 1,500 feet, forests are exceedingly

Table 3. Numbers of higher plant species present in Micronesia.

===

PLANT CATEGORY	NATIVE			INTRODUCED	OVERALL TOTAL
	ENDEMIC	NOT ENDEMIC	TOTAL		
Ferns	31 (16%)*	167	198	9 (4%)**	205
Gymno-sperms	0	1	1	18 (95%)	19
Monocots	166 (45%)	201	367	308 (46%)	677
Dicots	369 (56%)	293	662	680 (51%)	1,342
TOTAL	566 (46%)	662	1,228	1,015 (45%)	2,245

===

SOURCES:

F. R. Fosberg, M.-H. Sachet, and R. Oliver, 1979, 1982, and 1987.

* Endemic percentages are percents of Total Native for each category
     (e.g., 31/198=16%).
** Introduced percentages are percents of Overall Total for each
     (e.g., 9/205=4%).

mossy with vascular epiphytes, and above 2,000 feet trees are stunted.

The forests of Pohnpei are the most extensive in Micronesia. Small sawmills have operated there since the turn of the century. Such mills might also be found in Kosrae and Palau.

The residents of Pohnpei are noted for their use of *sakau*, the *kava* of Micronesia. This drink is the squeezings of the pounded roots of a pepper shrub, *Piper methysticum*. The commercial growth of black pepper corns was initiated in the 1960s and is still pursued.

The topography of Kosrae is similar to that of Pohnpei, as is its vegetation. Kosrae's upland forests, too, are comparable to those of Pohnpei with some of the same species dominant (i.e., *Cyathea ponapeana*). Some others are endemic, among them the tree *Horsfieldia nunu*. As on Pohnpei, but unlike elsewhere in Micronesia, the highest forests are mossy and stunted.

The high islands of Chuuk lagoon, Yap, and Palau also feature mangroves, strand communities, and highly disturbed coastal plains. All of these islands have some remnants of primary forest at higher elevations. Yap and Palau also have extensive grasslands. The vegetation on the famous "rock islands" of Palau is basically undisturbed. (See Photo 4, page 17.) The preferred betel-nuts (*Areca cathecu*, family *Palmae*) of all Micronesia are grown in Yap.

The Mariana Islands extend in a north-south arc, with rainfall decreasing northward. The vegetation of Guam is the best known of any of the high islands of Micronesia. In 1970 the flora of

Photo 1. Typical coastal vegetation of Micronesia, low trees and shrubs, e.g., *Messerchmidia* and *Scaevola*; coconut palms often grow slightly behind above plants, northwestern Guam, Mariana Islands.

Photo 2. A waterway cut into mangroves of Tol Island, Chuuk, FSM.

Photo 3. Secondary forest around a small ranch in the uplands, rain forest in background, Pohnpei, FSM.

Photo 4. The undisturbed vegetation of a small "rock island" in the Chelbacheb area, Palau, western Caroline Islands.

Guam comprised 931 species, 327 of which were classed as indigenous.

In northern Guam some forests remain on the elevated hard limestones. Because of their trimmed and shortened nature, the forests of this plateau have been called "typhoon forest." (See Photo 5, below.) Repeated exposure to typhoons has also eliminated most of the larger trees in the Mariana Islands. However, some exist in protected areas as seen in Photo 6, p. 19.

The southern volcanic mountains of Guam are mostly covered by sword grass (*Miscanthus floridulus*), with intervening ravine forests. (See Photo 7, page 19.) This grass often grows in dense, impenetrable stands. The origins of these grasslands are uncertain, but probably resulted from the limitations imposed by the dense, impervious, unstable, and clayey soils.

During the Japanese mandate, large areas of Saipan, Tinian, and Rota were put to agricultural uses. World War II further disturbed large portions of the natural environment of Guam, Saipan, and Tinian as they were affected by military activities including bulldozing for air fields and storage sites. Following the end of WWII, many of the disturbed areas were seeded with *tangan tangan* (*Leucaena leucocephala*, the *ha'ole koa* of Hawai'i) and extensive thickets of this small tree remain today. Presently, urbanization affects ever-expanding areas of Guam and Saipan. (See Photo 8, page 20.)

As a consequence of these disturbances, natural vegetation is difficult to find in the southern Mariana Islands. Rota is the least disturbed of the four main Mariana Islands.

It may be argued that any endemic plant found on only one or two small islands is in threat of extinction. Explosive population growth and economic development, particularly on Guam and Saipan, increases the threat. Currently three species, *Serianthes nelsonii*, *Heritiera longipetiolata*, and *Cyathea lunulata* are officially listed as endangered. The first is a tree of the bean family of which only two mature individuals survive on Guam and perhaps 65 on Rota. The second, again a tree endemic in the Marianas, is but slightly less rare and is found mainly in some coastal areas. The third is a tree fern, which grows only on Guam and Palau. On Guam it is limited to remote ravine forests in the southern mountains. (See Photo 9, page 20.)

Photo 5. Bulldozing reveals the structure of this forest; pandanus, *P. fagrans*, is dominant; cycads, *Cycas circinalis*, are in the foreground, north-central Guam, Mariana Islands.

Photo 6. This uncommonly large tree (over 4 feet in diameter), *Intsia bijuga*, is sheltered from typhoon strength winds by cliffs, Tarague, Guam, Mariana Islands.

Summary

The flora of the Micronesian islands is limited to a relatively meager 1,228 indigenous species, of which 566 are endemic. Besides these, another 1,015 species were introduced, mostly after the first European contact in the beginning of the 16th century.

Large and ecologically diverse islands which are also well watered and located close to plant sources tend to contain the largest number of indigenous species. Conversely, small, dry, and remote islands are species poor.

The coastal vegetation of Micronesia tends to be formed by a small number of widely distributed plants. The interior areas of high islands contain large proportions of endemic species and due to their limited accessibility have retained more of their original vegetation.

Human activity has drastically altered the lowland regions of all inhabited islands to the extent that hardly any but those plants useful to man now occur there. Cultivation of crops has always been difficult because of poor soil conditions, insect pests, and the various rigors of climate. Urbanization on some of the main islands is now posing an additional threat to the flora.

Photo 7. Grasslands and ravine forests within the volcanic mountains of southern Guam, Mariana Islands.

Photo 8. A forest remnant growing on limestone cliffs, dominated by *Cynometra ramiflora*, northern Saipan, CNMI, Mariana Islands.

Photo 9. An association of betel-nut palms *(Areca cathecu)* and the endangered tree fern *(Cyathea lunulata)* growing in a ravine in the grasslands of southern Guam, Mariana Islands.

Prehistoric Settlements in Micronesia

The first human settlers in Micronesia probably were maritime-horticultural peoples migrating eastward from the Philippines and Indonesia. (See Figure 10, page 22.) Some scholars have suggested that the peopling of Micronesia began around 3,500 years ago; but the initial period of human settlement is just beginning to be explored by archaeologists, and remains of very early island occupation have thus far not been found. Current archaeological research indicates that all the high volcanic islands (Palau [Belau], Yap, Truk, Pohnpei, Kosrae, and the Marianas) were inhabited at least a thousand years before the beginning of the first century A.D. The prehistory of the Micronesian coral islands (the Carolines, Gilberts, Marshalls, and Nauru) is even less known than that of the high islands.

The high islands and many of the coral islands were densely populated when first visited by European explorers in the 16th century. Successful cultural adaptations by the islanders had resulted in a diversity of languages and socio-political organizations throughout the region.

Linguists divide the languages of the area into a "nuclear Micronesian" group - referred to here as the Oceanic group (Carolinian, Trukese, Pohnpeian, Kosraean, Gilbertese, Marshallese, and Nauruan) - and the more diverse and possibly older languages of the Rimlands or the "Western" group: Palau (Palauan), Yap (Yapese), and the Marianas (Chamorro). The latter three are thought to have had their origins in an ancient language called proto-Austronesian.

Socio-political organization in Micronesian societies varies from flexible kinship groupings, with simple ranking of clans, to less flexible and more stratified chiefdoms with hereditary more stratified chiefdoms with hereditary social classes. Some of these socio-political organizations encompassed more than one island and linguistic group, such as Yap and several of the coral islands to the east.

Micronesian native technologies are specifically adapted to local conditions. Living in villages and homesteads, the islanders are successful tropical farmers and fishermen, as well as frequent sea-voyagers and traders using outrigger canoes. The inhabitants of the coral islands are more mobile than those of the high islands, in response to droughts, storms, population pressures, and food-gathering needs.

Archaeological remains found on many Micronesian islands in recent times represent the late prehistoric and early historic period populations. On the high islands, there are remnants of stone house platforms and compounds, public and private ceremonial and religious sites, and many acres of canals, ditches, and modified stream-courses, as well as numerous garden terraces and pondfields. Some of these features are still in use, although most were abandoned sometime after European contact in the 19th century.

The famous ruins of Nan Madol in Pohnpei, a sacred residential and ritual complex built of large basalt "logs" on more than ninety artificial islands, date from the late prehistoric period, starting Figure 10. Prehistory and Settlement in Micronesia around A.D. 1000. Other megalithic sites from this prehistoric era have been found on Palau, Yap, and Kosrae. In the Marianas, the large building foundation posts, or *latte*, are comparable to the stone house platforms on other islands. The present native populations of Micronesia are the descendants of those who built and used these sites.

On the coral islands, archaeologists have found prehistoric pavements, graves, and foundations of dwellings and meeting houses constructed of coral blocks and gravel. Refuse deposits containing shells and fishbones, associated with these features, exist as well.

The Order of Settlement

Human settlement of the low coral islands of Micronesia may have occurred after the more habitable or inviting high volcanic islands had been occupied. The volcanic islands were larger, had better soils, and consequently offered greater scope for agricultural endeavor. In addition, the high islands were less susceptible to the damaging effects of tropical storms than were the coral islands. Thus, high islands offered more stable, more secure, and potentially more productive environments to the early settlers than did the smaller coral islands.

Prior to their permanent settlement, some coral islands may have been exploited by the inhabitants of nearby high islands in limited ways, such as for seasonal harvests of sea turtles and as resting places during long-distance canoe voyaging. Archaeological work in the coral islands so far has been limited to a few test excavations, which have

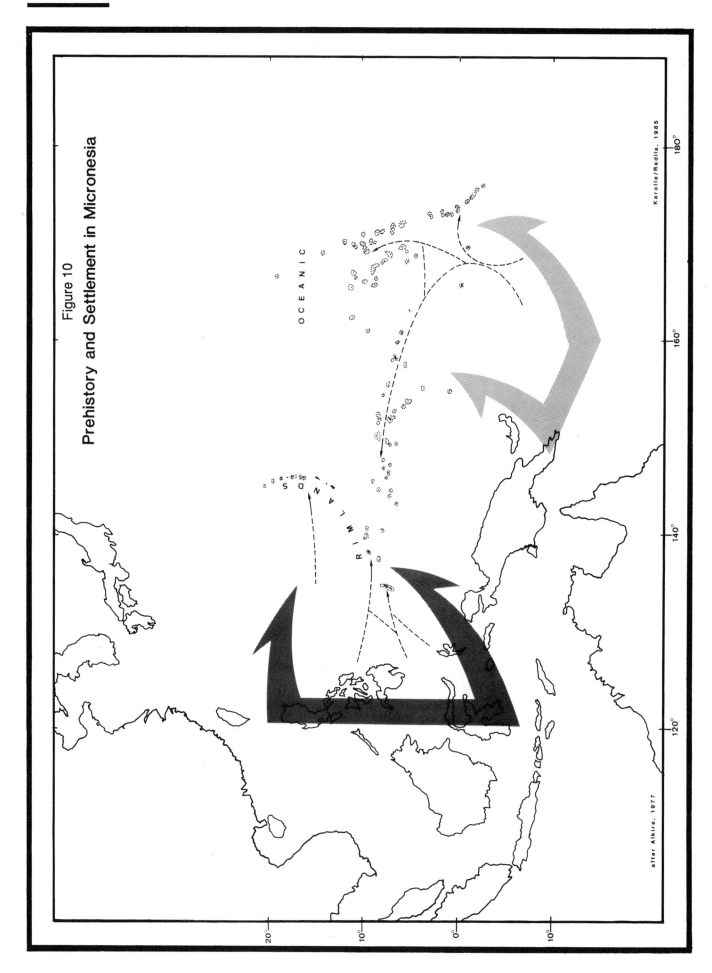

Figure 10
Prehistory and Settlement in Micronesia

after Aikire, 1977

Karolle/Redila, 1985

not revealed much about specific activities that may have taken place there. Therefore, it is not known whether and to what extent the excavated remains represent temporary or permanent settlements. As in the case of the volcanic islands, no very early deposits have been discovered.

In the absence of archaeological remains from the earliest periods of human habitation in either the coral or the volcanic islands, physical anthropologists and linguists have constructed various scenarios for the order of Micronesian settlement on the basis of present language and racial variations. One of these scenarios, suggested by the physical anthropologist William Howells, postulates a northern route of migration into the area. According to Howells, peoples from the Philippines and Indonesia around 6,000 years ago settled the high islands of the Carolines (Palau, Yap, Truk, Pohnpei, and Kosrae) and the Mariana archipelago. As these first populations grew and land became relatively scarce, offshoot groups migrated again to the coral islands in the east, west, and south. According to this scenario, the last islands to be occupied in Micronesia were those not already occupied in the eastern and central sectors: the Gilberts, the Marshalls, and the non-volcanic Carolines.

Another scenario, or postulation, favored by William Alkire, pictures at least two source areas and migration routes contributing to the major original populations of Micronesia. The first was a migration source (and route) similar to that suggested by Howells: the Philippines and Indonesia. These areas provided settlers for the Rimlands - Palau, Yap, and the Marianas. A second migration originated from the south, in eastern Melanesia. This source provided settlers first in the Oceanic islands of the Gilberts and the Marshalls, then into the eastern Carolines - Kosrae and Pohnpei. Next to be settled were the central Carolines - Truk and the nearby non-volcanic islands. Eventually, according to this theory, these people voyaged further westward, bypassing the already-occupied high islands of the Marianas, Yap, and Palau, to settle the small coral islands such as Sonsorol, Pulo Anna, Merir, and Tobi. Alkire's model is mainly based on linguistic analyses comparing Micronesian languages with others in the larger Pacific region, as depicted in Figure 10.

The prehistoric Micronesians (pre-A.D. 1500) transformed their island landscapes through the introduction of economically useful plants such as coconut, breadfruit, taro, and yams. They also introduced several animals, including rats, chickens, and dogs. Some native animals, birds, and plants may have become extinct as a consequence. All the high islands of the Carolines and the Mariana archipelago have yielded artifactual deposits dating to several hundred years prior to A.D. 1; dated sites in the coral islands tend to be later.

On the high islands, natural shorelines were deliberately altered by the inhabitants as their numbers increased, and land was used more intensively. They dug pondfields for taro cultivation and constructed large stone fish traps, weirs, and piers of several different kinds. They altered shorelines by building stone sand entrapments, and they increased the land area on which taro could be grown through the careful placement of stone seawalls to prevent salt-water intrusion.

On the coral islands, similar shoreline alterations were used to regain land lost after typhoons had eroded portions of it and to join smaller islets to create larger islands. Such activities indicate a sophisticated understanding of physical processes in small island settings and an ability to work with nature rather than against it.

Early Historic Contact and Exploration in the Pacific and Micronesia

The first European to sight and record the name of the Pacific Ocean was Vasco Nuñez de Balboa in 1513. He first saw the Pacific from what is now known as the Republic of Panama, at a site located about 8 degrees north latitude on the Gulf of Panama. Balboa named the great ocean *Mar del Sur*, or the Southern Sea.

This occurred long after the original settlement of the Pacific realm. The major insular regions of the Pacific - Melanesia, Micronesia, and Polynesia - were settled in prehistoric times. The exploration and mapping of the Pacific had to wait until ship-building and navigational skills had advanced to the point where sailing out of sight of land for extended periods no longer involved unacceptable risks. It had, by then, also become possible to record with some accuracy the routes followed and locations visited.

It would appear that the inhabitants of the Asian coasts and the off-shore islands along the western boundary of the great ocean had no great curiosity as to what lay beyond their more distant eastern horizons. They were probably satisfied with coastal and inter-island settlement and trade. The North and South American peoples along the eastern boundary of the Pacific Ocean apparently took even less interest in the sea beyond their offshore fishing grounds, and they developed neither the vessels nor the curiosity about the sea that might have spurred them to venture beyond sight of land.

Spanish Lake: The Early Years

In 1521, Ferdinand Magellan made the first trans-Pacific crossing in about fourteen weeks. According to Magellan's chronicler, Antonio Pigafetta, the great navigator started out on November 28, 1520, from the end of the Southwest Passage of the Straits of Magellan, which he had discovered and explored at that time, and sighted Guam (or Rota) on March 6, 1521. His Pacific Ocean route covers a distance of approximately 10,000 miles, and, interestingly, Magellan saw only two small uninhabited islands before arriving at Guam in the southern Mariana Islands. (See Figure 11, Magellan's Pacific Route, page 25.)

The objectives of the Magellan Expedition, and the eventual circumnavigation of the globe, centered on finding a direct ocean route from Europe to Asia by traveling westward. The popular paradigm at that time, in the late 1490s and early 1500s, was based on the Ptolemaic world map. Ptolemy's world, in 130-150 A.D., was considerably smaller longitudinally than the nearly correct global circumference outlined by Eratosthenes in Alexandria 400 years earlier. This east-west view indicated that India/China ended the world on the east and that Europe/Africa - and after Christopher Columbus, America - was the westward extent of the world. The notion that the American landmass extended to the south polar region and would prevent a sea voyage to the East Indies or China was widely accepted.

However, a few navigators, among them Christopher Columbus, held a different view. Ferdinand Magellan, a Portuguese, was willing to put it to the test. When Magellan's theory of a western passage to the East through some opening in the American barrier received no support in his own country, he turned to Spain, where he found the backing he sought. On September 20, 1519, Magellan sailed on his quest with five ships under Spain's colors. He reached the Brazilian coast and,

on December 13, anchored in Santa Lucia Bay, off what is now Rio de Janeiro. He worked south, exploring every bay, and finally entered the stretch of water which was to bear his name, as a fitting memorial to independent thought and courage. He spent thirty-seven days in the Strait, and lost two ships there. At last, on November 28, 1520, he sailed with his three remaining ships (*Victoria, Trinidad,* and *Concepcion*) past Cape Desire and entered the great Southern Sea. The voyage from Europe to the Pacific had taken over fourteen months, a period filled with suffering and conflict due to weather conditions, lack of food, mutiny, and shipwreck.

Magellan turned his course northward along the South American coast and what is now Chile, then west, inclining northward in his westerly progress. Thus he passed north of the Tuamotu Archipelago and south of the Marquesas. The seamen suffered so much from scurvy and hunger that a half ducat was paid for a fresh rat. Two small uninhabited islands were sighted, but provided no relief. After three months and some days of incredible hardship, the expedition arrived on March 6, 1521, at Guam in a group of islands which Magellan first named the Islands of Lateen Sails (*Islas de las Velas Latrinas*), after the canoe sails used by the natives. Later he changed the name to the Islands of the Thieves (*Islas de los Ladrones*) because of his view of the inhabitants' propensity for stealing. In the next century the islands were renamed the *Islas Marianas.* Today they are known as the Mariana Islands.

Following a three-day stay in Guam, Magellan sailed on to Samar, in the Philippines, taking only a week from Guam by following the northeast trade winds. Next Magellan reached Cebu, where he foolishly sided with a local rajah against the rebellious small island of Mactan off the east coast of Cebu. He and eight of his men were killed. The ship *Victoria,* under the command of Juan Sebastian del Caño, was the only vessel of the original fleet of five ships to return to Europe. The voyage ended in Seville, Spain, on September 8, 1522. Though most of the men and ships were lost, Ferdinand Magellan not only discovered a western passage to the Pacific through the Strait of Magellan, South America, but, by crossing the Pacific, determined that the global world embraced the Pacific Ocean, the world's largest body of water. He also put on the world map for the first time the rimland islands of the Ladrones

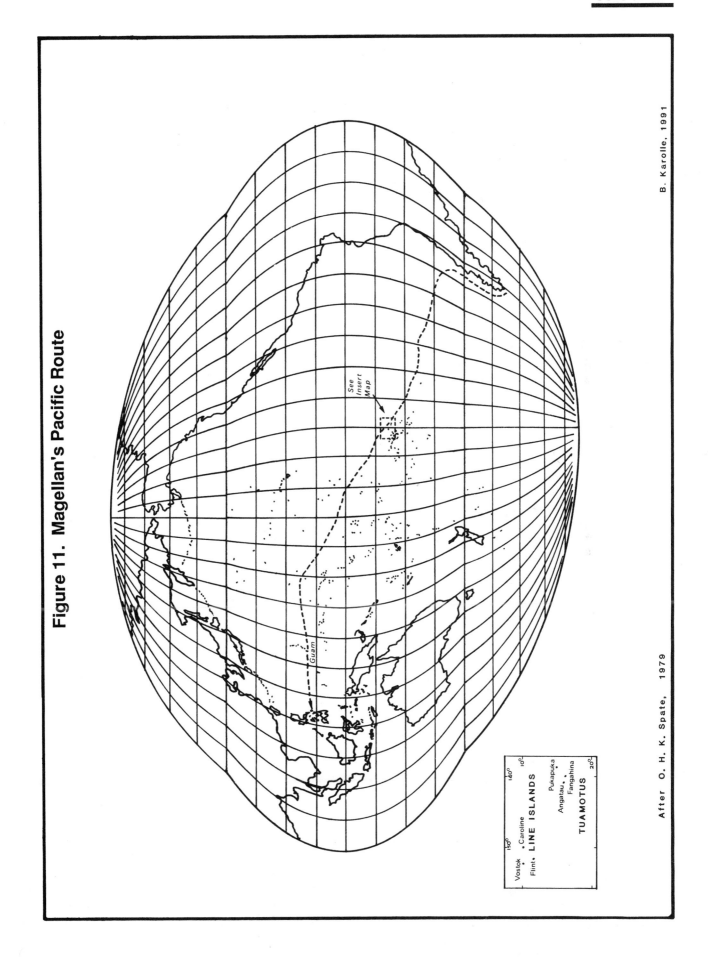

Figure 11. Magellan's Pacific Route

See
Insert
Map

Guam

LINE ISLANDS
Vostok
Caroline
Flint
150°
140°
10°

Pukapuka
Angatau
Fangahina
TUAMOTUS
20°

B. Karolle, 1991

After O. H. K. Spate, 1979

(Guam). The many other small islands of the region would be discovered and recorded, one by one, and named, collectively, Micronesia, by Domeny de Rienzi in 1831.

Post-Magellan

While del Caño led the *Victoria* westward back to Spain to complete the great Captain-General's mission, the ship *Trinidad*, under Captain Gonzalo Gomez de Espinosa, returned to the Ladrones from the Spice Islands (Moluccas). On the way Espinosa discovered Sonsorol, a Southwest Island of Palau. (See Figure 12, page 28, which shows the major discovery routes of the earliest known explorations in Micronesia.) Thinking it a short journey, Espinosa was trying to cross the Pacific to the Isthmus of Panama. Storms in the northern Marianas aborted this attempted voyage. However, an islander, perhaps from Agrihan, was taken aboard. Later, somewhere in the Marianas, the native and three crewmen abandoned the *Trinidad*. A surviving sailor, Gonzalo de Vigo, stayed four years. He made his way to the southern Marianas, Rota or Guam, where he was picked up by a ship of the Loaysa Expedition in 1526 (Garcia Jofre de Loaysa commanded the second Pacific voyage from Spain, 1525-26). An apprentice pilot on the Loaysa ship, Andres de Urdaneta, would return with Miguel Lopez de Legazpi in 1564-65. In the intervening years, information about the Ladrones was most likely passed on by Vigo to Urdaneta in 1526, providing the place-names and charting information about the newly discovered Pacific seas and territories for the maps of that period. According to Marjorie G. Driver, some 74 ships called at Guam and Rota between 1521 and 1602. This was 66 years before the missionization (1668-98 of Guam and the Marianas led by Father Sanvitores, who gave the islands their present name.

Table 4, page 27, lists the navigator(s) or expedition(s) and the islands discovered or charted during that period. The compilation highlights only the major voyages through Micronesia in these early times, according to Driver, Spate, Hezel, Buck, and others.

Following the second Spanish trans-Pacific voyage by Loaysa, New Spain (Mexico) became the point of departure for crossing the Pacific Ocean to the Spanish Philippines, via Guam. In the 16th century, Spain and Portugal vied for the East Indies (Indonesia). Portugal was successful in the Spice Islands and Spain gained the Philippines. In this early period and during the process of consolidation and continuing competition for insular Southeast Asia, trans-Pacific exploration was based in New Spain, the center of Spanish Pacific operations. Several expeditions led by such captains as Ruy Lopez de Villalobos (1542), Alvaro de Mendana (1567-69), and Pedro Fernandez de Quiros (1596) provided navigational data and left their mark in the region of Micronesia as they journeyed to and from Indonesia and Mexico. (See Figure 12.)

The Spanish galleon trade from Mexico to the Philippines was an annual voyage, usually by one cargo galleon and an escort, leaving Acapulco, Mexico, in the spring. The ship was loaded with Mexican and Peruvian silver bound for Manila, Philippines, traveling by a westward route following the North Equatorial Current and the easterly trade winds. The ships would require about eight weeks to cover the 8,000 miles to Guam, where they called mainly for water and food.

The galleons had to make the crossing from Guam to Manila as speedily as possible in order to acquire the Oriental treasures of spices, gold, etc., and leave before the late summer typhoons. The return route for these trading ships was the northern passage, or the route northeast through the Philippine Sea past Japan into the westerly wind belt across the Pacific Ocean aimed for the California coast. On the last leg of this journey, the galleons traveled south along the California coast past Baja to Acapulco in hopes of arriving before Christmas.

The Spanish empire would dominate the Pacific in general, and Micronesia in particular, for the next two hundred years in terms of exploration and trade, as well as in political and religious affairs. But Spain's interest lay on both sides of a vast ocean and this allowed a great number of others to sortie into the region. Ships of other nations discovered, rediscovered, named and renamed, charted and recharted Micronesian seas and any number of the many islands. (See Figure 13, page 29, R. Vaugondy's 1764 *Les Isles*, a map indicating parts of western Micronesia.)

English navigators were the first to challenge Spanish domination. It was Francis Drake who first discovered Palau. Thomas Cavendish, in 1587, reached Guam on his circumnavigation. But significant British exploration of Micronesia did not take place until the 18th century with such notable voyages as Woodes Rogers' in 1710; George Anson's in 1742; Norton Hutchinson's in 1761; Philip Cartaret's in 1767; and Henry Wilson's in 1783.

The Dutch would pass though early, but posed no real threat to the Spanish. Captain Olivier van Noort stopped at Guam and possibly Rota in 1600, and Gheen Schapenham passed through Micronesia in 1625.

The earliest American captains to pass through Micronesia were Thomas Read, 1787, and Benjamin Page in 1798. Serious interest began in the early 1800s with the arrival of Captains Scott Jenkes in 1802; Samuel Boll in 1804; and, the best known, Edmund Fanning in 1808-09. But it was whaling and missionary interests, from the 1840s onward, that brought relatively large numbers of Americans into Micronesia.

Important scientific surveys by other nations included the voyage by Louis Freycinet of France, in 1819, to explore and describe the land and people of the Marianas. Other notable French expeditions that produced a wealth of information in this period were those of Louis Duperrey in 1824, and Dumont d' Urville in 1828. Interestingly, the Russian Captain Fedor Lutke, who came to explore and map the Caroline Islands in 1828, left his legacy in Pohnpei, which he called the Senyavin Islands, a name still in use today.

Yet some of the greatest names in the exploration of the Pacific are absent from the Micronesian area. The great navigators like Vitus Bering, Abel Tasman, and James Cook - to name a few - never ventured into Micronesia. In more recent times, exploratory and cartographical efforts by individuals have been overtaken by

Table 4. Early Exploration/Discovery in Micronesia
(1521-1579)

NAME	ARRIVAL DATE/COUNTRY	ISLANDS	PURPOSE
Ferdinand **Magellan** *1st Pacific Voyage*	1521 (Spain)	Ladrones Guam/Rota	Discovery; resupply
Gonzalo Gomez de **Espinosa**	1522 (Spain)	Tobi/Sonsorol Palau; Guam	Discovery Shelter & supplies
Diogo da **Rocha** (& Sequeira)	1525 (Portugal)	Ulithi/Yap	Discovery
Garcia Jofre de **Loaysa** *2nd Pacific Voyage*	1526 (Spain)	Bokaak (Taongi), Marshalls; Guam	Discovery; resupply
Alvaro de **Saavedra** Ceron	1528 (Spain)	Rongelap/Ailinginae, Marshalls; Fais, Yap; Pohnpei (Ponape)	Discovery
Alvaro de **Saavedra** Ceron	1529 (Spain)		Discovery
Miguel Lopez de Legazpi	1564 (Spain)		Resupply
Spanish annual galleon trade commences:	1565 (Acapulco, Mexico [New Spain] to Manila, Philippines)		Galleon shipping
Fray Andres de **Urdaneta**	1565 (Spain)		Resupply
Alonso de **Arellano**	1565 (Spain)		Discovery
Francis **Drake**	1579 (England)		Discovery

Figure 12. Post-Magellan Exploration in Micronesia

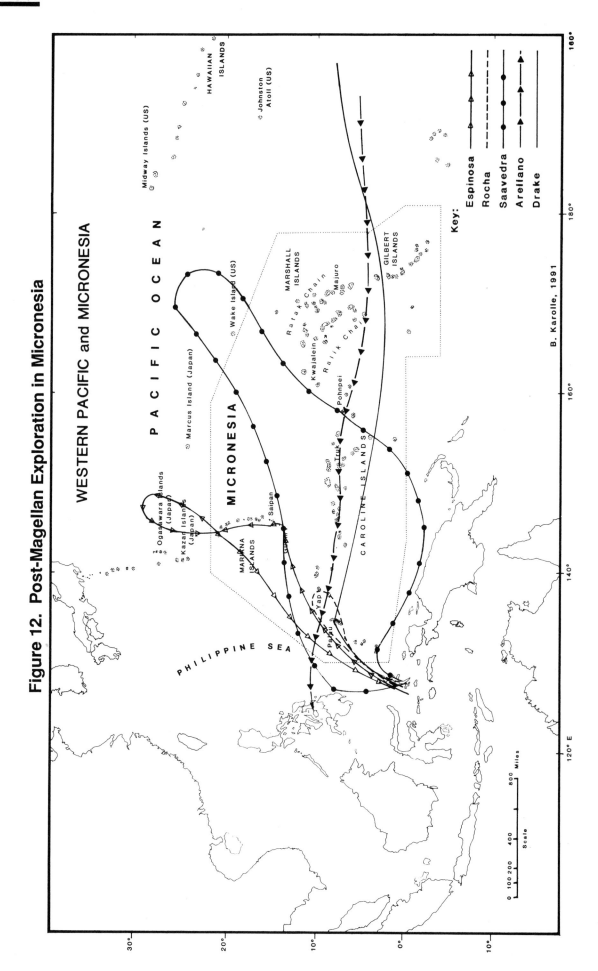

WESTERN PACIFIC and MICRONESIA

B. Karolle, 1991

technological progress, which has lent new dimensions to these fields of inquiry. The process of scientific mapping of land and oceans is now accomplished through the use of photogrammetry and satellite imagery, and continues in Micronesia as well as in other parts of the world. Thus, the making of geographic renditions of the Micronesian region and its many tiny islands is an ongoing pursuit.

Foreign Rule: 1668 to 1945

Micronesia and the entire Pacific were opened to the West in 1521, when Ferdinand Magellan stopped at Guam during the first circum-navigation of the globe. This visit established the Spanish claims to the Marianas; however, no settlements of any consequence were made until 1668, when the Jesuit missionary Father Diego Luis de Sanvitores established a colony on Guam.

Spain

Sanvitores vigorously Christianized the natives of the Marianas, whom he referred to as Chamorros. In 1669 the first school was established to teach the catechism, writing, reading, and arithmetic. It was called "el Colegio de San Juan de Letran." Within three years, Sanvitores claimed to have baptized 50,000 islanders. It is doubtful whether so many people were converted, or even existed on the island at that time. Whatever the number may have been, however, it is clear that Sanvitores was successful enough to become involved in local island political rivalries. The records indicate that a Chinese named Choco resented Sanvitores

Figure 13. *Les Isles*

enough to incite the islanders against him by claiming that the holy water used by the priests was poison and that those baptized would die.

The pressure of the Spanish eventually led to fighting and bitter disagreements among the missionaries, the native islanders, and the foreigners such as Choco. In 1672 Sanvitores was martyred near Tumon Beach by a Chamorro named Matapang. Supposedly he was killed because he insisted on baptizing a dying infant against the wishes of the parents.

The friction between the missionaries and the Chamorros continued to worsen and led to a series of three "Chamorro wars" between 1672 and 1700. During this period, Don Jose Quiroga, the governor of the Marianas, succeeded in subduing the rebels by chasing them into the hills - or off to other islands such as Rota and Saipan - and pursuing them until they became Christianized. This activity greatly reduced the Chamorro population, and by 1700 the census showed fewer than 2,000 were left. They had been lost due to diseases, the wars, and forced relocations.

During the years between 1565 and 1815, Guam and other islands of the Marianas became regular stops on the Spanish trans-Pacific galleon trade, which passed yearly between Mexico and the Philippines. This trade stimulated the economy of the islands, but the people did not really prosper. A succession of Spanish governors were sent from Madrid to "los Indios," as the islands were sometimes called.

After 1850, the Spanish empire, once the greatest in the world, began to rapidly crumble. In June 1898, Captain Henry Glass arrived at Guam aboard the American ship *Charleston* to sink any Spanish ships that might oppose the American attack on Manila. Instead of any active Spanish force, Glass found a sleepy island whose governor was not even aware that his country was at war with the United States. The "Spanish Lake" was no more.

After the Spanish-American War of 1898, the Marshalls, Carolines, and Marianas were all sold to Germany for $6 million. The United States retained Guam as a naval base to support the Philippines, which had become an American colony following the Spanish-American War.

Germany
The German administration was short-lived but vigorously motivated to develop the islands economically and agriculturally. The main seat of the German colonial administration in the Pacific was in New Guinea. Within Micronesia, there were five sectors established, each with its own governor: Saipan, Yap, Truk, Pohnpei, and the Marshalls.

A large center was established at Pohnpei to undertake experiments and demonstrations in tropical agriculture. There were impressive agricultural stations established on the other islands as well. The Germans also built dispensaries and schools. The schools were run by German Catholic priests and also by Lutheran missionaries. There were no government schools except for one at Saipan. The Germans had difficulty getting colonists to come from Germany to settle in the Pacific, so their administration was never characterized by large numbers of expatriates. Typhoons, droughts, floods, and insects plagued the German efforts, and they were never able to realize profits from their colonial efforts in Micronesia.

Japan
In October 1914, with the start of World War I, the Japanese swept through Micronesia, except for Guam and the Gilbert Islands, and seized all the German administrative centers. Great Britain similarly seized the German lands south of the equator, and so the German political, economic, and military presence in the Pacific vanished within a few weeks. The German colonials in Micronesia were quickly interned and then sent home; thereafter, the Japanese established a naval administration throughout the islands. The Japanese kept the same basic geo-political organization the Germans had established, but also added Palau as an administrative center.

The Treaty of Versailles, which ended the war, provided that all the German lands north of the equator would be ceded to Japan as a kind of "war spoil." The United States, however, regarded the Japanese presence in the North Pacific as a strategic threat to the Philippines and Guam. The U.S. insisted that Japan join the League of Nations and administer the islands through the mandates system, and this Japan agreed to do.

In 1920, after the awarding of a "class C mandate" to Japan, a civil administration was established in the islands, with the seat of government located in Palau. The Japanese promoted the most vigorous economic development that had ever been seen in the islands. They also brought in large numbers of homesteaders to develop the agricultural potential of Micronesia. The extensive economic development was designed mostly for the Japanese themselves, and their social aims were to "Japanize" the Micronesians. The school systems established were the most comprehensive ever introduced; the Japanese language was the main part of the curriculum. Only the first three grades were required, with the option of two extra years for promising students.

In 1935, Japan withdrew from the League of Nations after a series of criticisms and questions about its administration were raised. The metropolitan powers of the Pacific had become concerned about Japan's secrecy regarding Micronesia. After 1935, the islands came under the control of the Japanese military once again, and they began to prepare for war. Hostilities in the Pacific began on December 7, 1941, when units of the Imperial fleet attacked the American fleet at Pearl Harbor, Hawaii. Simultaneously, the Philippines and were also seized and the Pacific phase of World War II began. In a series of bloody battles between 1942 and 1944, the American forces captured the Japanese strongholds in Micronesia, and by October 1944 all the islands were secured by the Americans. Immediately following WWII, all the Japanese nationals in Micronesia were repatriated, and the economies of the islands collapsed completely.

American Micronesia

The motivation of the American presence in Micronesia following WWII was strategic and not acquisitive. The Americans arranged for the former Japanese areas of Micronesia to be administered by them under the United Nations, which was the successor to the League, as a "strategic trust." The Trusteeship Agreement with the United Nations was signed by President Harry S. Truman on July 1, 1947, and established the Trust Territory of the Pacific Islands (TTPI). In 1951, following the signing of the Japanese Peace Treaty, the United States changed the federal authority for the administration of the islands from the Navy to the Department of the Interior.

For the first fifteen years of the American administration, not much happened in the way of economic development or investment. Schools were established as well as hospitals; but these were not adequate, nor were they up to the vigorous standards that had been previously set by the Japanese. Political development, although democratic by nature, was very slow. The main American interest in those early years of administration remained military, and several sites in the Marshall Islands were used as testing grounds for a series of thermonuclear explosions, mainly at Bikini Atoll. These military tests decimated environments, harmed people, and caused possibly indelible damage to the islands used as targets.

After 1962, under the Kennedy administration, more vigorous development programs were undertaken. More schools were built, and educational programs were accelerated. More funds were made available for various economic development programs. Some infrastructure was started. In 1965, the Congress of Micronesia was established together with a series of local island legislatures. In 1969, political status negotiations were begun between the Micronesians and the United States to determine future status. During the administration of President Gerald Ford, a status of "free association" was mutually decided upon. This was a new status within the American political scheme. It called for each island group to be autonomous and self-governing while having a "compact of free association" - a treaty - to govern its relationships with the United States. The islands of Micronesia then divided themselves into three freely-associated states and one commonwealth of the United States, as follows:

TTPI	POST-TTPI
Marianas district	Commonwealth of the Northern Mariana Islands
Yap district	Federated States of Micronesia (FSM)
Truk district	FSM
Pohnpei district	FSM
Kosrae district	FSM
Palau district	Republic of Belau
Marshalls district	Republic of the Marshall Islands

Each of the new island political entities has a constitution that provides for its internal self-government while the compacts and the covenant for the commonwealth provide for their relationships with the U.S.

Beginning in the late 1970s and early 1980s, programs to promote tourism on a larger scale began and a number of first-class hotels were built in Saipan, Rota, Palau, and Truk. The Japanese have invested particularly heavily in these tourism activities, as they have also done on Guam.

Guam has remained an unincorporated territory of the United States since the Spanish-American War of 1898. It has an Organic Act instead of a constitution. Guam is currently pursuing preliminary negotiations with Washington to seek improvements in its status along the lines of the agreement already reached by the Commonwealth of the Northern Mariana Islands.

Nauru

Nauru is not included in American Micronesia, but it is culturally and geographically a part of the region. It was settled by various Gilbertese, Carolinians, and Marshallese in pre-contact times. The Europeans came in the late 18th century, and it soon became a regular stop for whaling ships. German businessmen came in the 19th century, and in 1888 they incorporated it into their Marshall Islands Protectorate. The discovery in 1898 of high-grade phosphate on Nauru has today made the Nauru people among the most prosperous in the entire region. In 1967, Nauru, as a Trust Territory of Australia, New Zealand, and Great Britain, gained its independence. The government has established the Nauru Phosphate Royalties Trust in order to protect the people's high standard of living when the phosphate runs out.

Kiribati

Kiribati, formerly known as the Gilbert Islands, is also culturally and geographically a part of Micronesia, but not politically a part of the American flag areas. Kiribati actually comprises three island groups: the Gilberts, the Line Islands, and the Phoenix Islands. It has the largest water area of any of the new Pacific countries. The Europeans arrived in the 16th century, and, as they became more established, the islands of Kiribati became a regular area for whaling. In the 19th century, the islands were a favorite haunt of slave

traders (blackbirders), who sold the natives as plantation laborers in Australia and elsewhere. Today, phosphate and copra are the main exports. In 1877, Great Britain established a high commission in Kiribati, and it was a Crown Colony until it attained independence on July 12, 1979.

American Expansion into the Pacific

The United States emerged onto the world stage in 1867 following the American Civil War. During the half-century from 1867 to 1917, there occurred a period of intense international rivalry among the industrialized powers in Asia, Oceania, and elsewhere, of which the United States took full advantage. Specifically, American ideas of economic development had manifested themselves since the 18th century, and by the 1840s whaling interests, along with religious missionaries, had attracted Americans to Micronesia. But dissension between the northern and southern states, culminating in the Civil War of 1861 to 1865, brought territorial expansion to a halt. Prior to this great upheaval, the U.S. Congress had passed the Guano Act of 1856, which authorized Americans to assert the proprietary claim of the United States government to any unoccupied islands for the purpose of mining guano. Eventually, under this act, some forty-eight islands were claimed, most of them located in the Pacific Ocean. Only four of these Pacific islands remain in U.S. possession today. (See Figure 14, page 34.)

When this forward movement resumed at the end of the U.S. Civil War, industrialism and later finance capitalism combined with an earlier type of empire-building that had stressed commerce and territorial aggrandizement. This new foreign policy manifested itself in a war against Spain in 1898, a watershed year in which the United States plunged into world politics. Meanwhile, it had strengthened its Navy and occupied strategic outposts before claiming supremacy in the Pacific as well as in the Caribbean.

The first step in the resumption of American westward movement was the acquisition of Alaska in 1867 as the result of a deal with Czarist Russia. To many Americans, Alaska was both the back door to Canada and the geographic link to Asia. With the Aleutian archipelago stretching out toward Japan, Alaska was considered a "natural bridge" to northeast Asia.

Since the mid-19th century, Hawaii had been

the main jumping-off-point to the Orient. A three-power rivalry involving Britain and France had kept American relations with the native kingdom in an unsettled state, but with the annexation of Midway Island in 1867, the United States moved ahead of the other two powers. A commercial treaty signed in 1875 made Hawaii a virtual American protectorate, and in 1887 the United States obtained Pearl Harbor as a coaling station and future naval base. Annexation entered its final stage in 1893, when a group of sugar planters and Honolulu businessmen, aided by American officials, overthrew the native monarchy and established a republic. Formal annexation occurred in 1898.

Other territorial annexations followed Hawaii. Wake Island was annexed in 1899. Earlier, in 1878, a foothold had been established at Pago Pago in the Samoan group, where the British and Germans were also involved. Friction was resolved by a treaty (1899) partitioning the group into American and German possessions, but the Germans lost their share to New Zealand in 1914.

The main island acquisitions of the Spanish-American War in the Pacific were the Philippines and Guam, both formally ceded by Spain under the peace treaty of 1898. The United States now had its "stepping stones" to China, already the focus of international rivalry as a field for capital investment.

American Rule In Guam

On June 20, 1898, the United States naval vessel *Charleston* sailed into Guam's Apra Harbor. Although the Spanish-American War had begun two months earlier, the Spanish garrison on Guam had not yet been informed. The *Charleston* secured control of the island by firing ten warning shots, which were taken for salutes by the Spanish. Through an exchange of messages with the governor, the surrender took place the next day. The acquisition of the Philippines and the formal annexation of Hawaii in the same year marked the emergence of the United States as a full-fledged colonial power.

Initially envisioned as a coaling station, Guam never became more than a small auxiliary naval station during the next forty years. Indeed, there was some confusion in Washington as to whether Guam or the entire Mariana archipelago of fifteen island units had been acquired. In 1906, a wireless station was installed. By 1914, coaling stations were obsolete, and despite some calls for a buildup during World War I, few fortifications were constructed on the island. The Washington Disarmament Conference of 1921 led to the demilitarization of Guam during the inter-war period.

A conservative Roman Catholicism continued as the major foreign influence in Guam, although the Navy did improve health services and established a rudimentary education system. There was also significant entrepreneurship by the Japanese, who were present in relatively large numbers building the economy of the nearby northern Mariana Islands. While the 1908 census showed only 101 Japanese residents in Guam, many were involved in the most significant trade and commerce of the island. It was not until 1935, when Pan American World Airways began its trans-Pacific China Clipper service from Alameda, California, to Manila, that Guam was opened to American travelers. As revealed in Roger W. Gale's dissertation, in comparison with the neighboring islands, Guam remained an undeveloped, unutilized island. "A pity!" lamented one writer, "the largest and most fertile of all these islands and not used. While Guam's exports have been about $100,000 annually, those of Saipan, half its size, have been, under Japanese management, four times as large."

On December 8, 1941, the same morning as the surprise attack on Pearl Harbor, Japanese aircraft from Saipan, 115 air miles to the north, attacked Guam. By the next day, a Japanese invasion force was marching down the island's main road, and the garrison, which numbered less than 500 soldiers, had surrendered. Seventeen Americans, one Guamanian, and one Japanese were killed. In 1938, Rear Admiral Arthur Hepburn, Commander in Chief of the United States Fleet, had advocated a major military buildup on the island. Shortly before the outbreak of the war, a decision had been made to fortify the island, but it obviously had not yet been implemented by the time the war broke out.

Figure 14. United States Expansion in the Pacific Ocean

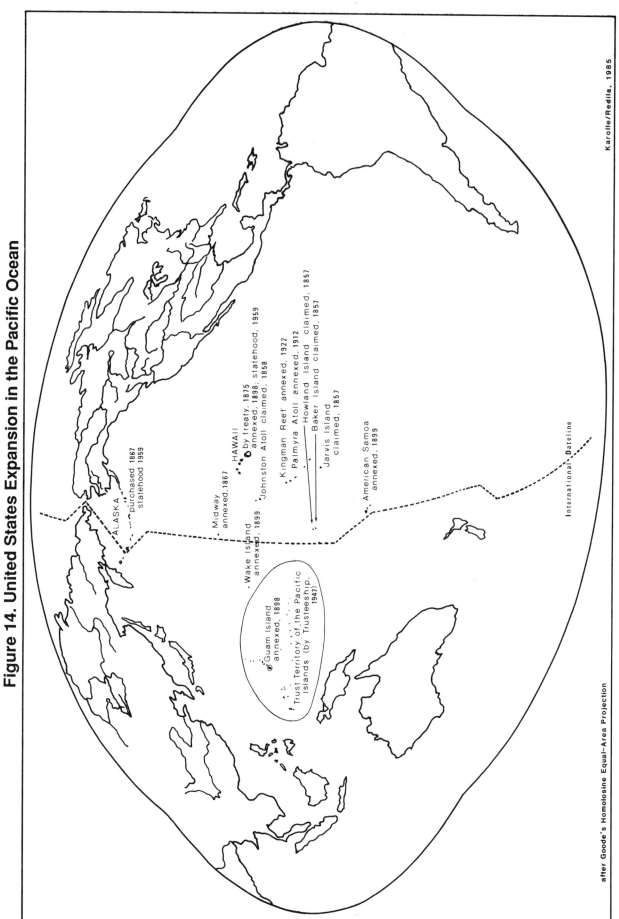

ALASKA
purchased 1867
statehood 1959

Midway
annexed, 1867

HAWAII
by treaty, 1875
annexed, 1898; statehood, 1959

Johnston Atoll claimed, 1858

Kingman Reef annexed, 1922

Palmyra Atoll annexed, 1912

Howland Island claimed, 1857

Baker Island claimed, 1857

Jarvis Island
claimed, 1857

American Samoa
annexed, 1899

Wake Island
annexed, 1899

Guam Island
annexed, 1898

Trust Territory of the Pacific
Islands (by Trusteeship,
1947)

International Dateline

Karolle/Redila, 1985

after Goode's Homolosine Equal-Area Projection

PART 2 - MICRONESIA

Introduction

This section of the atlas devotes specific attention to Micronesia by showing spatial characteristics of the entire region at one time. The regional map encompasses the entire geographic area of Micronesia based on the U.S. Geological Survey 1973 Lambert projection. In addition to the first maps in the series (Figure 15, 15a, and 15b, pages 37-39), which indicate the locations and names of the main islands and atoll units as indicated by numbers in Table 5, page 41, and defined in the "Island Unit List," pages 42-44, selected features and regional characteristics of demography, economy, and climate are shown.

Figure 16 (page 46) indicates population size and distribution based upon ten areal partitions of Micronesia. The map shows the major human settlement variations within the region, and the color/pattern code contrasts the averaged populations by area. The original toponymics (place names) of Figure 15 are overprinted to help identify individual islands.

The section on traditional canoe travel found in the central Caroline Islands focuses on two isles as shown in Figures 17 and 18 (page 49). Figure 19 (page 52) is a rendition of the navigational chart utilized in their system of canoe voyaging.

The section on economic development reviews the past and present resources of the region. Figure 20 (page 52) shows the high mark for exports of the former TTPI. Figures 21 and 22 (pages 56 and 57) indicate the importance of marine resources. Each political entity's national oceanic boundaries are shown as 200-mile exclusive economic zones (EEZ). Figures 21 and 22 also repeat the base map place names, which remain overprinted for easy identification of the separate areas. Figure 22 indicates overall export earnings from EEZ fishing reported by the new states. Nauru's phosphate exports make it an exceptionally wealthy island nation.

Two new sections have been added to show or indicate the development of tourism and distant education. The economics of both have tremendous impacts on the American Micronesian areas.

Figures 29 through 34 (pages 74 through 81) show climate patterns and weather characteristics of the region. Also indicated are individual weather data by station as well as the cyclone tracks of two great typhoons of the last twenty years.

On the pages following Figure 15 and Table 5 is a list of the current place names of the islands, indicated as geographical "units," and shown in Table 5, column a. Most of the names listed are also found in their correct geographic positions in Figure 15. Those names not shown in Figure 15 are identified as such by the symbol ^ in the listing. An asterisk (*) indicates that the island unit is an atoll. However, there are many variant spellings and names for places throughout the region.

Photo 10. Coastal high island: reef and road

Restoration of Indigenous Geographic Names in Micronesia

The emergence of Micronesia from foreign control in the past twenty-five years has given rise to restoration of indigenous geographic names. In many instances this has been reflected in spelling changes to make them more representative of actual pronunciation. In other cases the original local names have been reinstated in place of those created by foreigners.

Some foreign names have had to be retained, because the indigenous ones were lost, such as in the case of the Mariana Islands. A list of names accorded by foreigners to various localities in Micronesia between 1521 and the mid-19th century presents a picture of considerable confusion. Commonly the same place was given different names by different explorers who were unaware of the cartographic efforts of their predecessors.

Another source of error was the practice of asking the inhabitants of a certain island the names of other, more distant ones. The names learned in this way, while correct in the language of the informants, often were unknown to the people of the islands in question. The explorers themselves, being of many different nationalities, naturally adopted differing orthographies for the names they learned. This became another source of confusion.

Finally there are instances of islands being named, in disregard of local appellations, for distant monarchs (the Marianas), ships' captains (the Marshalls), crew members (Pitcairn Island in Polynesia), scenic features, or contemporary personalities of one sort or another.

A review of the more notable and more recent of these shifts in nomenclature reveals the extent of the problem.

Nauru

Nauru was named "Pleasant Island" in 1798 by a British captain. So it remained for about a century until the indigenous name was probably restored by the Germans in the late 1890s.

Kiribati

The Russian cartographer A. I. Krusenstern named this group the Gilbert Islands for a British captain who sighted some of the islands in 1788. The indigenous name of the archipelago was, and still is, Tungaru.

When the Gilberts became independent from Britain in 1979, the Line Islands and Phoenix Islands were incorporated into the new country. A new name had to be adopted because the new state now comprised a much larger area beyond Tungaru. "Kiribati," being the closest Gilbertese approximation to "Gilberts," was chosen. As there is no "s" in Gilbertese, like in many other Micronesian languages, the "ti" had to fill that function.

The pronunciation of Kiribati thus is "Kiribous" with the "a" sounding like a short "u" and with the stress on the first syllable.

The Marshall Islands

The Marshall Islands, to the north of Kiribati, were named by the same Russian mapmaker for the captain of another ship on the same voyage.

There is no Marshallese name for the group as a whole, other than "our islands," but the two island chains that together constitute the Marshalls are called "Ratak" and "Ralik," meaning "Sunrise" and "Sunset." If the Marshallese were ever to contemplate a name change for their country, "Republic of Ralik-Ratak" would be the most likely alternative. The individual atolls here all bear their correct names. The northern atoll of Bokaak had been called Taongi until its name was restored in the 1980s.

The Marshallese Islands have a claim to Wake Island, which is called "Enen-kio" in Marshallese, meaning "Island of the Orange Flower," but a bill pending in the United States Congress would transfer control of that territory to Guam rather than to the Marshalls.

Kosrae

None of the Micronesian island names is more frequently mispronounced than that of Kosrae. The island was once called "Ualan." Subsequently it became "Strong's Island" and eventually "Kusaie."

The current spelling was introduced after the islanders gained control over their own affairs in the 1980s. Kosrae should be pronounced as "Ko-shae", with the "ae" representing a long "i" and the "sr" standing for "sh".

Pohnpei

A notable change in Pohnpei State was the recent modification of Mwokil to Mwoakilloa, which was

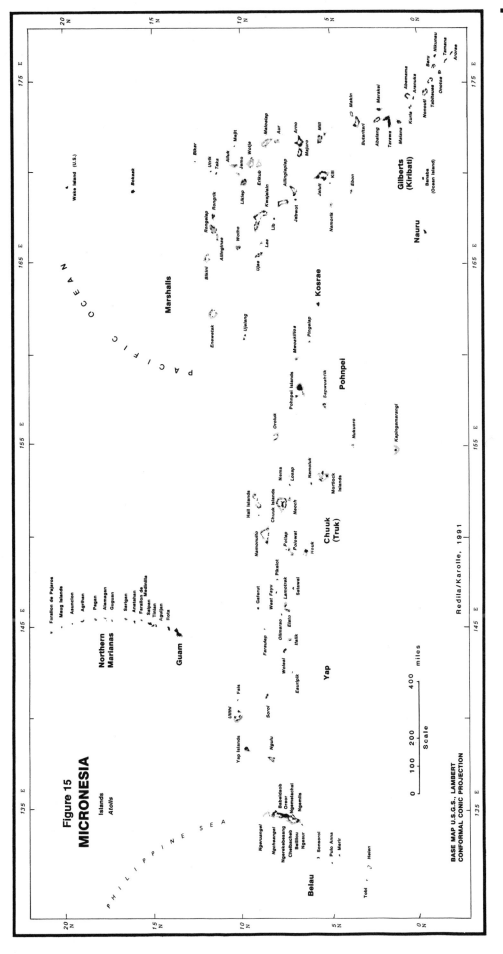

Figure 15

MICRONESIA

• Islands
⌐ Atolls

**BASE MAP U.S.G.S., LAMBERT
CONFORMAL CONIC PROJECTION**

Redila/Karolle, 1991

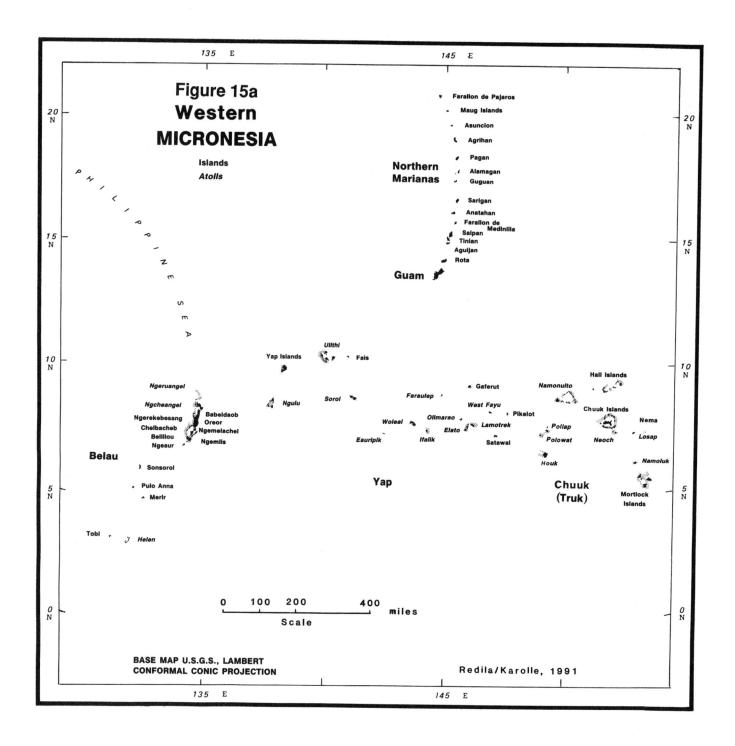

Figure 15a
Western
MICRONESIA

Islands
Atolls

BASE MAP U.S.G.S., LAMBERT
CONFORMAL CONIC PROJECTION

Redila/Karolle, 1991

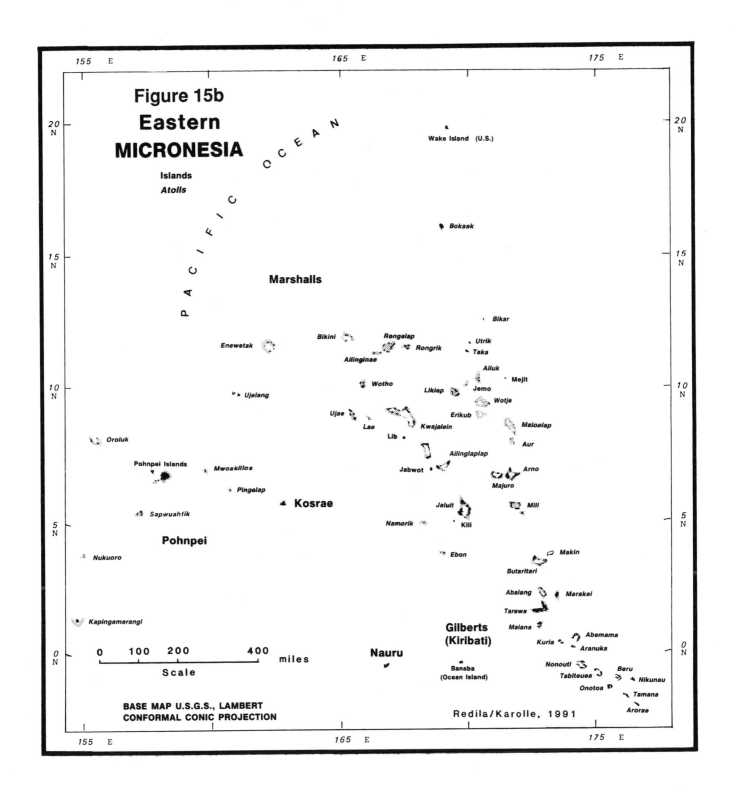

Figure 15b
Eastern
MICRONESIA

Islands
Atolls

PACIFIC OCEAN

Wake Island (U.S.)

Bokaak

Marshalls

Bikar

Bikini   Rongelap
Enewetak   Rongrik   Utrik
Ailinginae   Taka
                              Ailuk
Wotho   Mejit
Ujelang   Likiep   Jemo
                         Wotje
Ujae   Erikub
    Lae   Kwajalein   Maloelap
Oroluk   Lib   Aur
Pohnpei Islands   Mwoakilloa   Ailinglaplap
          Pingelap   Jabwot   Arno
                              Majuro
Sapwuahfik   Kosrae   Jaluit   Mili
                         Namorik   Kili
Pohnpei
Nukuoro   Ebon   Makin
                         Butaritari
                    Abaiang   Marakei
Kapingamarangi   Tarawa
                    Maiana
0 100 200   400 miles   Kuria Abemama
        Scale   Aranuka
                    Nauru   Nonouti   Beru
BASE MAP U.S.G.S., LAMBERT   Banaba   Tabiteuea   Nikunau
CONFORMAL CONIC PROJECTION   (Ocean Island) Onotoa   Tamana
                    Redila/Karolle, 1991   Arorae
Gilberts
(Kiribati)

the traditional form of the name. Likewise Ngetik has reverted to Sapwuahfik.

Pohnpei itself has also undergone a series of namings and renamings. The Spaniards called it "Ascension Island," but at least five other names were bestowed on it by successive explorers, until it came to be called Ponape. This was fairly close to the current spelling of Pohnpei (long "o" in the first syllable). The name means "Upon a Stone Altar" and refers to a local creation legend.

Chuuk

Chuuk, which rhymes with "duke," known for many decades as "Truk," has seen a veritable avalanche of name changes, as many of the designations introduced by outsiders were essentially wrong. Chuuk means "mountain" in Chuukese and refers to the Chuuk Lagoon, where the mountainous high islands are located.

Most of the other islands of Chuuk State are small, low coral atolls. The inhabitants of the outer atolls do not normally consider themselves Chuukese, except in an administrative sense and in dealing with outsiders who are not expected to grasp subtle distinctions of this order.

By 1879 the "tr" spelling appears on maps, probably introduced by the Germans, although they pronounced "Truk" as "Chuuk," unlike the British and Americans to whom it read "Truck." After a century of coping with a succession of foreign languages, from Spanish to German to Japanese and finally English, the islanders came up with a solution whereby "Chuuk" is "Truk" in dealings with foreigners and "Truk" is "Chuuk" among the Chuukese. Regrettably, now that Chuuk is the official name, many islanders find it awkward when speaking English and there is a trend to revert to "Truk."

The main island of the Chuuk Lagoon, called Moen by outsiders, has had its original name of "Weno" restored. It is pronounced with "e" as in "fed" and "o" as in "book." Moen was the name of the village on Weno called "Mwan."

The real name of the island of Dublon, meanwhile, is "Tonoas" (both "o"s long and the "a" short). "Dublon" was the name of a ship's captain who visited Chuuk in 1814.

The Mortlock atolls to the south of Chuuk Lagoon have been known by that name for so long that their indigenous designations have been lost. John Mortlock was a ship captain whose name was given not only to these islands, but to the Takaus in Papua New Guinea as well.

Another sailor, John Hall, lent his name to the Hall Islands to the north of the Chuuk Lagoon. They are known as "Namonpafeng" (meaning Northern Islands) by the locals.

The Western Islands of Chuuk are known as "Namonpattiw." Of the better known islands whose names have been changed in recent times, mention is made of Pollap, which used to be Pulap, Polowat, formerly Puluwat, and Pulusuk, which has become Houk, pronounced to rhyme with "Coke."

Yap

There are a number of anecdotal accounts of how the name "Yap" originated, including one in which a question about the island's name is mistaken as one about a canoe paddle, but the facts seems to be that "Yap" is the Woleaian and Satawalese name for the island the Yapese call "Waab." This name, again, originally applied only to the largest of the four islands of the Waab group.

Palau

Some years ago Palau was changed to Belau (pronounced Bay-lau, with the stress on the first syllable). The Belauans have apparently adopted a two-name policy, with "Palau" being used when English is written or spoken and "Belau" when Belauan is the medium.

Although "Palau" is acceptable, "Belau" is the proper, official and preferred spelling. An antiquated rendering of the word is "Pelew."

The Marianas

Geographic names in the Mariana Islands have undergone numerous changes, from being called "Islands of the Lateen Sails" as well as "Islands of Thieves" by Magellan in 1521 after the inhabitants of these Islas Ladrones had relieved him of some of his possessions.

"Islas Ladrones" endured until the late 17th century, when the name was changed to Mariana Islands, in honor of the contemporary Queen of Spain, at the behest of the missionary San Vitores. As the Chamorro culture was virtually wiped out by the Spaniards, knowledge of the indigenous nomenclature is very scanty. Different names were applied to the same localities by different authorities at diverse times.

Guam, for example, has been known as "Guahan" and "Boan," with several other

Table 5. Geographical Area of Island Groups of Micronesia*

NAME	NUMBER OF ISLANDS		SIZE IN SQUARE MILES	TOTAL SQUARE MILES BY POLITICAL TERRITORY
	a # of units	b # of individual islets/reefs		
Federated States of Micronesia				
Yap	16	149	45.925	
Truk	12	290	49.181	
Pohnpei	8	163	133.364	
Kosrae	1	5	42.316	
			SUBTOTAL: FSM	270.786
Belau	20	350	190.655	190.655
Marshalls	33	1225	69.840	69.840
N. Marianas	14	20	184.508	184.508
			SUBTOTAL: TTPI	715.789
Guam (U.S. territory)	1	1	214.000	214.000
			TOTAL: American Micronesia	929.789
Nauru	1	1	8.200	8.200
c Kiribati				
Banaba (Ocean)	1	1	2.417	
Gilberts	16	16	104.919	
			TOTAL: Kiribati	107.336
			TOTAL:Dry-land area of Micronesia	1,045.325

Sources: a. Motteler, 1986.
b. Bryan, 1971.
c. Tarawa Teacher's College, 1976. Note: Figures do not include
Line and Phoenix islands in Kiribati.
* Karolle, 1981.

Island Unit List
(Short Gazetteer of Micronesia)

I. Northern Mariana Islands, Commonwealth of the Northern Marianas (U.S.)

1. Rota (Luta)
2. Aguijan
3. Tinian
4. Saipan
5. Farallon de Medinilla
6. Anatahan
7. Sarigan
8. Guguan
9. Alamagan
10. Pagan
11. Agrihan
12. Asuncion
13. Maug Islands
14. Farallon de Pajaros (Uracas)

II. Guam, unincorporated Territory of the United States

III. Palau Islands, Republic of Belau

1. Ngeruangel* (Ngaruangl Reef)
2. Ngcheangel* (Kayangel)
3. Babeldaob (Babelthuap)
4. Oreor (Koror)
5. Ngerekebesang (Arakabesan)
6. Ngerchaol (Ngargol) ^
7. Ngemelachel (Malakal)
8. Chelbacheb (Rock Islands)

   a. Ulebsechel (Auluptagel) ^
   b. Ngeteklou (Gologugeul) ^
   c. Bukrrairong (Kamori) ^
   d. Ngeruktabel (Urukthapel) ^
   e. Tlutkaraguis (Adorius) ^
   f. Butottoribo ^
   g. Ongael ^
   h. Ngebedangel (Ngobasangel) ^
   i. Ulong (Aulong) ^
   j. Mecherchar (Eil Malk) ^
   k. Bablomekang (Abappaomogan) ^
   l. Ngerukeuid (Orukuizu) ^

9. Ngemlis (Ngemelis Islands)
10. Ngercheu (Ngergoi) ^
11. Ngedbus (Ngesebus) ^
12. Ngerechong (Ngeregong) ^
13. Ngebad (Ngabad) ^
14. Beliliou (Peleliu)
15. Ngeaur (Angaur)

Southwest Islands of Belau

1. Sonsorol Islands

   a. Fana ^
   b. Sonsorol

2. Pulo Anna
3. Merir
4. Tobi
5. Helen* (Helen Reef)

IV. Federated States of Micronesia

State of Yap

1. Pikelot
2. Satawal
3. West Fayu*
4. Lamotrek*
5. Elato*
6. Olimarao*
7. Gaferut

8. Faraulep*
9. Ifalik* (Ifaluk)
10. Woleai*
11. Eauripik*
12. Sorol*
13. Fais
14. Ulithi*

15. Yap Islands (Waqab)
   a. Rumung ^
   b. Maap (Map) ^
   c. Gagil Tamil ^
      (Gagil-Tomil)
   d. Yap ^
16. Ngulu*

State of Chuuk (Truk)

1. Mortlock Islands (Nomoi)

   a. Satowan* (Satawan) ^
   b. Lukunoch* (Lukunor) ^
   c. Etal* ^

2. Namoluk*
3. Losap*
4. Nema (Nama)
5. Hall Islands

   a. Murilo* ^
   b. Nomwin* ^
   c. Fayu ^

6. Chuuk (Truk) Islands

   a. Weno (Moen) ^
   b. Tonoas (Dublon) ^
   c. Eten ^
   d. Uman ^
   e. Fefen (Fefan) ^
   f. Siis (Tsis) ^
   g. Parem ^

   h. Totiu (Tarik) ^
   i. Eot ^
   j. Udot ^
   k. Ramanum (Romonum) ^
   l. Fanapanges ^
   m. Tol group ^
      Tol ^   Pata ^
      Wonei ^   Polle ^

7. Kuop* (Neoch) ^
8. Namonuito*
9. Pollap* (Pulap)

10. Polowat* (Puluwat)
11. Manila Reef ^
12. Houk* (Pulusuk)

State of Pohnpei

1. Pingelap*
2. Mwoakilloa* (Mwokil)
3. Pohnpei Islands (Ponape Islands)

   a. Pohnpei (Ponape)
   b. Ant* ^
   c. Pakin* ^

4. Sapwuahfik* (Ngetik)
5. Oroluk*
6. Minto Reef ^
7. Nukuoro*
8. Kapingamarangi*

State of Kosrae

   1. Kosrae (Kusaie)

V. Nauru, Republic of Nauru

VI. Marshall Islands, Republic of the Marshall Islands

Ratak "Sunrise" Chain   Sequence: North to South

1. Bokaak* (Taongi)	6. Ailuk*	11. Maloelap*
2. Bikar*	7. Jemo	12. Aur*
3. Utrik* (Utirik)	8. Likiep*	13. Majuro*
4. Taka*	9. Wotje*	14. Arno*
5. Mejit	10. Erikub*	15. Mili*
		a. Knox* (Narik) ^

Ralik "Sunset" Chain   Sequence: South to North & West

1. Ebon*	7. Namu*	13. Rongrik*
2. Namorik*	8. Lib	14. Rongelap*
3. Kili	9. Kwajalein*	15. Ailinginae*
4. Jaluit*	10. Lae*	16. Bikini*
5. Ailinglaplap*	11. Ujae*	17. Enewetak*
6. Jabwot	12. Wotho*	18. Ujelang*

VII. Gilbert Islands, Republic of Kiribati

1. Makin*	7. Abemama*	13. Nikunau*
2. Butaritari*	8. Kuria*	14. Onotoa*
3. Marakei*	9. Aranuka*	15. Tamana*
4. Abaiang*	10. Nonouti*	16. Arorae*
5. Tarawa*	11. Tabiteuea*	
6. Maiana*	12. Beru*	

Banaba (Ocean Island)

* designates atoll
^ indicates name omitted on Figure 15

appellations having been current at varying times. What may have been the name of the island prior to the appearance of the Spaniards in 1521 it is now impossible to ascertain.

Following the Spanish-Chamorro Wars of the late 17th century, the remnants of the indigenous population were removed to Guam from the Northern Mariana Islands, which remained uninhabited for more than 100 years. Settlement there was again permitted in the early 19th century, when both Chamorros from Guam and Carolinians evacuating storm-damaged islands established themselves on Saipan and Tinian.

The name Saipan occurs on a map dated 1544 and could therefore be an original Chamorro term, although Carolinians believe that the name means "empty journey" (sai peun in their language). This is said to have been because they found the island uninhabited in the 18th century.

The name Rota island is undoubtedly Spanish, relating to the Philippines. The Chamorro inhabitants call their island Luta as did Carolinians

Table 6. Population and Area of Island Groups in Micronesia, 1984 and **1990***

NAME	TOTAL POPULATION	SIZE IN SQUARE MILES	POPULATION DENSITY
Federated States of Miicronesia	88,375 **(90,761)**	270.786	326 **(335)**
Yap	10,595	45.925	231
Truk	44,596	49.181	907
Pohnpei	26,922	133.364	202
Kosrae	6,262	42.316	148
Belau	13,000 **(15,105)**	190.655	68 **(79)**
Marshalls	34,923 **(35,866)**	69.840	500 **(514)**
N. Marianas	19,635 **(43,555)**	184.508	106 **(236)**
SUBTOTAL: TTPI**	155,933 **(185,187)**	715.789	218 **(259)**
Guam (U.S. Territory)	119,000 **(133,152)**	214.000	556
SUBTOTAL: (American Micronesia)***	274,933 **(318,439)**	929.789	296 **(342)**
Nauru	8,400	8.200	1,024
Kiribati	62,503	107.336	582
Banaba (Ocean)	2,201	2.417	911
Gilberts	60,302	104.919	575
TOTAL	345,836 **(389,342)**	1,045.325	331 **(372)**

Sources: U.S.Department of State, 1984.
Pacific Islands Yearbook, 1984.
* Pacific Daily News, 1990 Census figures and an estimated growth rate of 2.7% per annum for the Marshalls & FSM
** States of the former Trust Territory of the Pacific Islands
*** Micronesian islands only; excludes Phoenix and Line Islands

Figure 16. Micronesia: Population

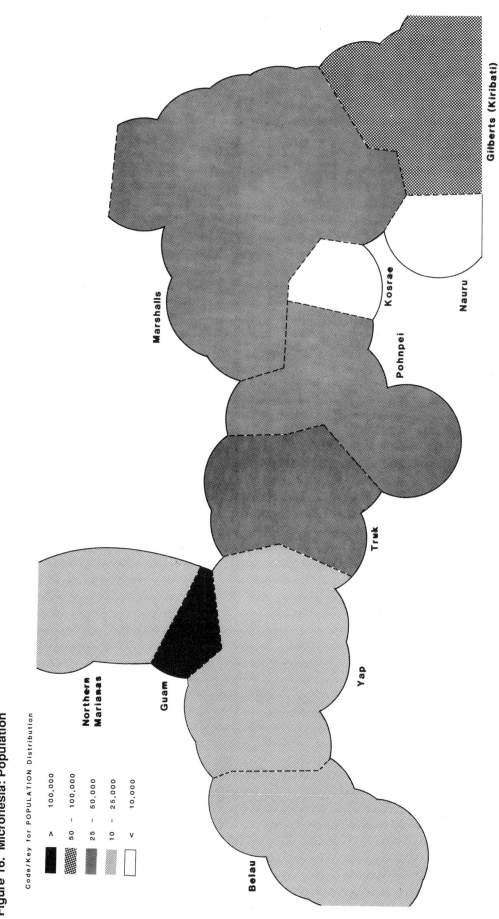

Code/Key for POPULATION Distribution

█	>	100,000
▦	50 –	100,000
▨	25 –	50,000
▨	10 –	25,000
☐	<	10,000

Northern
Marianas

Guam

Belau

Yap

Truk

Pohnpei

Kosrae

Marshalls

Gilberts (Kiribati)

Nauru

of long ago, although the meaning of the Carolinian term - "We have passed the small island" - is not the same.

In conclusion, Micronesians undoubtedly will continue the study of toponymy. The new states of Micronesia, as evidenced by the many name changes since the 1970s, demonstrate their interest in the restoration of indigenous geographic names to their islands.

Human Population Distribution

The population of Micronesia is unevenly distributed among the major island groups as well as between the two distinct physical island types, the high (volcanic) and low (coral) islands. (See Figure 16, page 46.) Population distribution, population pressures, and the ability of individual localities to support populations have changed continuously, but several important demographic patterns are discernible today.

Nearly eighty percent of the total population of the region lives in American Micronesia. (See Table 5, page 41.) The former Trust Territory of the Pacific Islands and Guam make up the American sphere of influence. The other independent states of Nauru and Kiribati (of which only the Gilbert Islands and Banaba are Micronesian) constitute eleven percent of the region's land area but contain slightly more than eighteen percent of its total population.

In 1984, Micronesia's total population was approximately 346,000. (See Figure 16.) Taking the actual area of dry land (1045.3 square miles or 2,707 km^2) into consideration, the single most important and recognizable man-land relationship, population density, becomes 331 per square mile, as indicated in Table 5.

Within the American sphere, the largest population concentration is found on Guam (the southernmost of the Mariana Islands), where a total of nearly 120,000 people live, accounting for forty-two percent of the inhabitants of American Micronesia. Guam is the region's largest island, and, not surprisingly, is the largest single population center in Micronesia, with nearly thirty-five percent of the total.

Compared with other Pacific island regions, Micronesia has a relatively high population density (the ratio of numbers of people per unit of land). For example, Hawaii has a population density of 150; French Polynesia - with a similar land size of 1,544 square miles and a population of

approximately 150,000 people in 1984 - has a density of slightly less than 100 people per square mile. Hence, Micronesia's population density is more than twice that of the State of Hawaii and more than three times that of the French Polynesian islands.

There are a number of other important population factors in Micronesia. First, not all islands are permanently inhabited. In areas where there are atolls and smaller coral islands, the inhabitants of other islands may intermittently use uninhabited islets and reefs for fishing and resource-gathering purposes. At present, more than half of all the islands in Micronesia are visited but uninhabited.

Second, modernization has created a number of spatial problems. Since World War II, economic development programs, increased use of land for military purposes, and urbanization have become determining factors in land-man relationships in Micronesia. Most of the State capitals (the former district centers of the Trust Territory) illustrate a shift toward urbanization. For example, Oreor (Koror), in Palau, has a land area of 3.6 square miles and had a population of 7,585 in 1984. This yields a density of 2,107 persons per square mile. Other highly populated centers are Moen, in Truk, with a population density of 1,966, and Majuro, in the Marshalls, with 3,600 persons per square mile. These concentrations are comparable to urban areas of Asia and North America.

Kwajalein Atoll, in the Marshall Islands, the world's largest atoll formation, comprising ninety-three islets, is the site of the U.S. Army missile base, located on Kwajalein islet, the southernmost of the group. Three miles due north, on Ebeye islet, where 8,500 Marshallese employees and their families reside, the population density was nearly 71,000 people per square mile in 1984. Ten years earlier, the population density at Ebeye was estimated at 51,000 per square mile.

Canoes and Navigation
in the Central Carolines

The Caroline archipelago stretches some 1,800 miles east-west between the fifth and tenth northern parallels of latitude. Today, there exist only two major sailing communities, on Polowat (Puluwat) and Satawal.

Polowat Atoll, situated on the western edge of Truk State in the Federated States of Micronesia (FSM), lies at approximately 7° 22' N. latitude. (See

Figures 2 and 15.) This atoll is composed of five islets: Polowat, Allei (Alet), Elangelap (Elangelab), To, and Sau. (See Figure 17, page 49.) It is just over two miles in length. More than two-thirds of this surface area is land. Between islands are a small outer lagoon area within the fringing reef and a second inner lagoon area which crescent-shaped Polowat islet almost encircles. The inner lagoon, further sheltered by Allei and Elangelap, is so well protected that canoes can be left moored there except during the most severe weather. To the southwest, the outer lagoon is protected only by a reef through which boats can pass to the open sea. From this atoll, the islanders still sail regularly to neighboring islands using traditional canoes and navigational knowledge.

Satawal is a raised coral island located approximately 125 miles directly west of Polowat in Yap State, FSM. (See Figure 18, page 49.) Unlike Polowat, the Satawal physical landscape provides little protection from the open ocean. The narrow fringing reef causes inhabitants and navigators alike several security and access problems; nevertheless, traditional navigation has survived into the present.

The low coral islands of the central and western Carolines share a similar culture and language. According to a Polowatese legend, the low islands were settled from Truk to the east, which, in turn, was settled from Pohnpei and Kosrae. More recently, the islands have been visited by explorers, traders, missionaries, and foreign administrators, who have stayed for relatively brief periods of time, intermittently, and have consequently influenced community life very little.

Although both are basically conservative, one notable aspect of the Polowat and Satawal societies is their willingness to adapt by accepting or rejecting new ways of doing things with confidence and very little agonizing. In general, these people are raised from birth with immense tolerance, acceptance, and affection, and they are quite self-confident both as individuals and as a group. They accept some new ways because they are easier, more useful, more sensible to them, and they reject other innovations for the opposite reasons. Thomas Gladwin, in *East Is a Big Bird*, gives the following Polowatese examples:

They disregarded determined German efforts to vest title to land in individuals, keeping it instead in matrilineal clans and smaller kin groupings with female descent. They accepted American insistence on the election of magistrates, but then allowed the magistrate power only over new programs and activities sponsored by the administration, reserving traditional matters for the traditional chiefs.

Local material for clothing, fishing supplies, and sails was readily discarded for Western cottons, nylons, and metals, but canoes are still built with breadfruit logs and coir rope lashings, as these are considered to produce a more sturdy, flexible craft. Many taboos and rituals surrounding activities related to the sea were dropped, although some customs remain with a different rationale: today women are still isolated when on canoes at sea for reasons of modesty and convenience rather than the earlier belief that they were anathema to the forces of the ocean.

Polowat and Satawal are forested with such useful trees as breadfruit, coconut, and pandanus. There are also gardens and taro swamps on both islands. People live near their boats in houses clustered near the shore.

There are probably enough canoes of all types to carry more than the total population (between 500 and 700 hundred people each on Satawal and Polowat in the 1980s). This canoe excess assures that transportation is readily available to almost anyone, especially in the case of Polowatese wishing to go by water across the lagoon on errands to the neighboring islands or even to the state capitals (former district centers). Borrowing customs are flexible: one need only ask the owner/owners of a canoe for permission, a formality hardly necessary with close relatives and friends.

The majority of the canoes in Polowat are small, single outrigger craft for use within the lagoon area. Made from a single breadfruit log, they are uncomplicated in design and ornamentation. They are from nine to twenty-four feet long and can carry from one to twelve people and their possessions. All canoes are individually owned, but they are usually kept in or near a canoe house - which is more than a club - and they are available to all the members. There are a few larger, usually by two or three feet, paddling-sailing canoes. Some of the smaller canoes are imported from the neighboring islands of Pulusuk and Pulap and, in the case of Satawal, from Lamotrek and Elato.

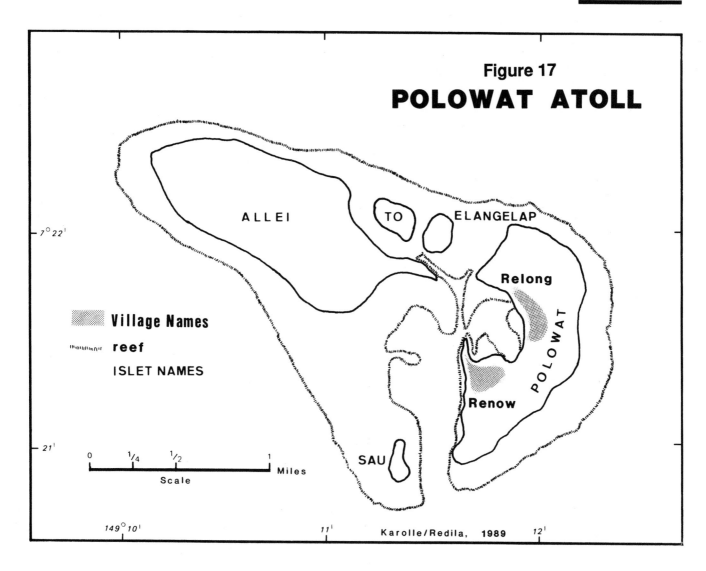

Figure 17
POLOWAT ATOLL

ALLEI   TO   ELANGELAP

Relong

POLOWAT

Renow

SAU

Village Names
reef
ISLET NAMES

7°22'

21'

0   1/4   1/2   1
Scale   Miles

149°10'   11'   Karolle/Redila, 1989   12'

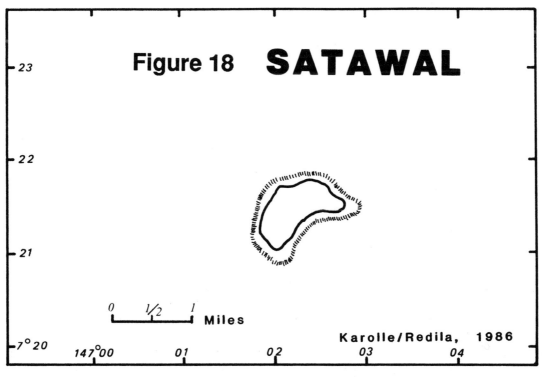

Figure 18   **SATAWAL**

23

22

21

0   1/2   1   Miles

7°20'   147°00   01   02   03   04

Karolle/Redila, 1986

Inter-island Sailing Canoes

Satawal and Polowat are known within Micronesia and to the Western world for their sophisticated long-distance sailing canoes and navigation skills. In mid-1976, the Satawalese traditional navigator, Pius Piailug, navigated the Hawaiian canoe *Hokule'a* on a one-month, 4,000-mile trans-oceanic trip from Hawai`i (Honolua Bay, Maui) to Papeete, Tahiti. In recent years, however, there also has been an overall decline in the traditional arts, crafts, and navigational techniques, and - mainly because of an increased reliance on government vessels and gasoline outboards - a marked decline in the traditional canoe exports from Polowat and Satawal.

Long-distance outrigger sailing canoes range between twenty-four and thirty feet in length. As in earlier times, they are built by master canoe builders and their apprentices, who know and learn the theory and practical skills of their craft as well as many magical rituals and spells. They also observe taboos against sexual activity and the eating of certain foods. Today, with the whole procedure less secret, all the members of a canoe house may help build a boat. These large canoes are used for open-sea fishing, inter-island travel, and trade. In earlier times, they carried tribute to Yap and colonists to other islands. Saipan, for example, was colonized from Satawal in the early 1800s. Warriors in sailing armadas were much feared in the central Carolines, and the Polowatese still make claims on Houk (Pulusuk) based on ancient conquests.

All sailing canoes are carefully maintained. Unless they are in constant use, they are beached and covered with mats to protect them from the drying heat of the sun, which can warp or crack the hull planks. When not in use, the canoes are kept off the ground on blocks inside canoe houses that shield them further from the weather. When they are left on the beach, they generally rest on palm fronds. Even inside the canoe houses, mats are tied around them to prevent drying by the wind. Sails are dried and stowed in the eaves of the canoe houses.

As art anthropologist Marvin Montvel-Cohen has observed, the canoe house itself is more than just a shelter for these vessels. It functions as a meeting house and workshop for the production and repair of fishing and sailing equipment. It is the center of the men's activities, and the canoes are visible symbols of their intertwined roles in society as fishermen, sailors, navigators, and builders of canoes. (The most important subsistence tasks of men and women are fishing and gardening, respectively.) Unmarried young men often sleep in the canoe houses and learn about their future roles. Many of the vital skills necessary for living in an island environment are taught at the canoe house. Informal court is held there to settle disputes, and news and gossip are also exchanged. Membership in a particular canoe house is usually determined by matrilineal ties.

The master canoe builders are often navigators as well; hence, they have more prestige than those with only one skill. The status of navigator is traditionally based on experience and ritual knowledge. According to Thomas Gladwin, the seniority of new navigators in Polowat today is somewhat ambiguous since the traditional initiation ceremony was discontinued in the late 1940s at the urging of a Catholic priest who objected to some of the sensual chants and prayers. These new navigators have less prestige than the older "initiated" ones, as do the men who would have gained honor by having trained them. This ceremony marked a man's total acceptance by his society and recognition as a master navigator by others in the elite group.

The Christians also belittled other traditional practices. Many taboos and rituals no longer exist because of the experiences of one of Polowat's foremost navigators, Winin. He decided that the only way to verify the priest's claim that the rituals and supernatural beliefs would not change the outcome of events or influence them would be to take a long voyage after ignoring all the traditional practices and taboos. He returned after a wonderful trip, and the islanders followed suit in discarding practices that were something of a nuisance anyway.

The Navigator and His Craft

Young men still apprentice themselves to a master, usually a relative. Training is rigorous, prolonged over many years, and involves instruction both ashore and afloat. It includes remembering and patiently observing the natural signs. The confidence at sea this schooling gives and the pride of the navigators is such that they will reportedly not even ask what island they have landed on when blown off course, as they feel they should know!

Satawalese and Polowatese navigators see the

ocean as being full of islands arranged in blocks or groups rather than widely spaced, isolated specks of land. The sea is viewed as a road, not a barrier, and one can journey forth confident that islands are sure to appear. There is no element of conquest in the attitudes of the navigators, and the lack of fear for generations in studying the conditions of the sea has made it a familiar, friendly place. These Carolinians respect the ocean, but feel confident that they can handle any situation by using their training and skill. Even drowning at sea is not viewed negatively, except perhaps by the families back home.

Navigation is characterized by its technological and cognitive dimensions. In the Carolinian system, the sidereal (star) compass is an abstract system of orientation by the horizon points where chosen stars rise and set. This "star" compass generally has thirty named points, with the North Star, Polaris, at the top of the compass circle, and the Southern Cross at the bottom. The bearings of stars at rising and setting are symmetrical; hence, most of the stars used in the "compass" indicate those two positions. The exception is Polaris, known to the Carolinians as the "star that does not move." Position, not magnitude, of a star determines its inclusion in the compass. The function of the stars is to indicate points around the horizon's rim. These points remain fixed whether the stars are visible or not, or currently in the appropriate position. The cardinal compass point and basis of the system is the point where Altair rises in the east. Altair passes very near the zenith of the Carolines, and while not in true east-west alignment, its use is solely as a reference. Everything is conceptualized with it, not with imaginary lines as in the Western system of parallels and meridians. Polaris and the Southern Cross upright are north and south. The Southern Cross is actually used for five of the positions on the sidereal compass, and constellations, not just stars, are used in the northern positions.

Etak is a concept of dividing up a voyage into stages or segments by the star bearings of a referent island. A navigator's position at sea is defined in *etak* terms. Carolinian training includes learning under which star (the direction) every known island is from every other one. One has traveled one *etak* (or segment of a journey) when the referent island has "moved" backwards by one star point (from one to the next) on the sidereal compass. (See Figure 19, page 52.)

The canoe is conceived as stationary beneath the equally fixed position of the stars and sun. The sea flows past, and the islands move astern. The Carolinian navigational system includes the memorization of all the bearings of islands to be visited from the point at which the navigator finds himself; he is always pictured at the middle of the action. If the canoe strays off course, the canoe is viewed as moving and the movements of the islands become temporarily irrelevant. Once back underway and heading along the correct seaway, the islands again slide by under the immobile stars.

Tacking uses the *etak* concept of invisible referents: the *etak* island referent is dropped and the destination substituted. Initial tacks are long; successive ones become shorter at each change so that near the destination the canoe is assured of intercepting the island. Tacks are made so many *etak* in one direction, then so many in the opposite. Most compensations for variables such as wind and wave interference are introduced early in each trip so that navigation en route can get the canoe close enough to its destination to find land signs or other visual sightings.

The concept of islands being located in blocks or "screens" is used by the Polowatese navigator to adjudge journeys easy or difficult. Deep reefs are important for extending the screens between and around islands. Wave patterns vary over a reef, and the color of the sea alters as well. Wave interference phenomena and normal wave patterns of the ocean swells are noted too.

Homing birds - noddies, white and sooty terns, and boobies - all act as reliable indicators of land between ten and twenty miles off. (At five miles you can often, weather permitting, see an island without any kind of instrument.) According to David Lewis, birds are found in the folklore of the Carolines too. On Pulap Atoll, just north of Polowat, it supposedly was a magic *kuling* (species of plover) that first revealed the secrets of navigation to mankind.

In addition to the villagers provisioning the canoe about to set out on a voyage, there are three major operational phases of Polowat navigation: 1) establishing initial course and sailing plan; 2) maintaining en route course and position (using the sidereal compass, *etak*, the sun, wave swells, and, more recently, the mariner's compass); and, 3) locating the destination (sailing into "screens," bird lore, reefs, and lying to).

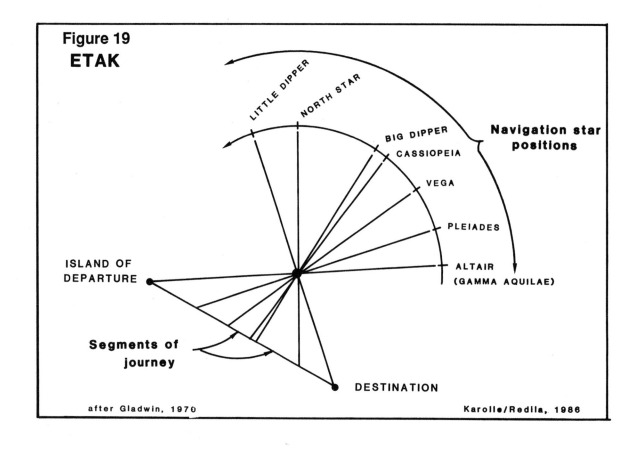

Figure 19
ETAK

after Gladwin, 1970   Karolle/Redila, 1986

Figure 20

TRUST TERRITORY
1980 Export Earnings

(Sector Estimates: US Dept. of State)
Annual Reports

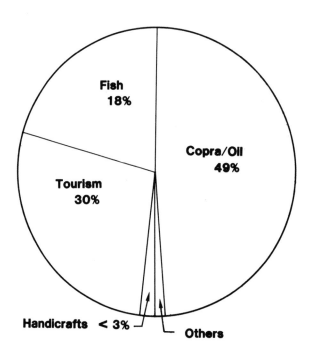

Future Navigation

What might the future hold for the traditional ways of voyaging in these central Carolinian islands? The following features of the traditional lifestyle are necessary for the old ways to survive beyond the current generation: retention of a social structure in which voyaging is an integral part; keeping the Carolinian art of navigation intact; and the availability of trained navigators to teach new men their art.

The economy of Polowat is gradually changing as more people leave subsistence living on the island for cash jobs elsewhere and new business and trade with others increases. Changes are being introduced by the emigrants. In the early 1960s, the head of Lefatu canoe house and his younger brother introduced motorboats to Polowat for the first time. Also at that time, tin and cement were introduced for construction purposes. Both changes were initially criticized, but soon they were copied by several families on the atoll, particularly those with members on government payrolls. As of August 1979, two of the approximately twenty canoe houses on Polowat were roofed with tin; the others were still covered in the traditional, locally available thatch. Inter-island sailing canoes were still going to other islands, but people were beginning to use the irregularly scheduled administration boats as well. There were about as many mechanized craft as traditional ones, and cement houses outnumbered thatch.

What will happen to the Carolinian navigation technology? David Lewis, in *We, the Navigators*, speculates that, as the magnetic and sidereal systems of orientation are so nearly incompatible, and since charts and compasses are far easier to master than sea lore requiring half a lifetime of laborious study, it seems certain that the Carolinian system will ultimately disappear and be replaced by the European. The use of a magnetic compass for secondary orientation is probably about the limit of modification the Carolinian concept will stand; in default then of the possibility of incorporation, it must eventually be supplanted.

The abandonment of the initiation ceremony for new navigators marked a decline in the formal recognition of the society concerning its special heroes. As the older master navigators die, it is these new, uninitiated men who must carry on the training. It may be that this diminished prestige will further erode the already limited respect for them as teachers. The ancient arts of navigation have died out in most parts of the Pacific. Perhaps the cultural pride of the people of Satawal and Polowat and their navigators can prevent the same thing from happening there.

Economic Development

Throughout Micronesia people traditionally earned their living by farming and fishing. Even today, many remain engaged in some way in a subsistence economy.

Past Economies

The indigenous subsistence economy began to be modified in the 16th century as a result of early commercial contact with Europeans. The history of economic impact by external factors may be divided into three periods:

1. China trade (1790 - 1850). Traders introduced Western goods such as ironware and cloth in exchange for beche-de-mer (dried sea cucumber), turtle shells, and shark fins. These products were exchanged for tea, silk, and other commodities in Chinese ports. This also was the period of the trans-Pacific Spanish galleon trade that established commercial exchange between Mexico and the Philippines. The Mariana Islands were regularly visited on these lengthy voyages.

2. Whaling ship trade (1840 - 1860). Several Micronesian islands became regular sources of supply for the whalers. In 1855, for instance, some forty whaleships called at Pohnpei and purchased approximately $8,000 worth of food, tobacco, timber, water, and other provisions.

3. Copra trade (1850 to the present). Commercial planting and processing of coconuts was begun during the brief period of German control and was continued and expanded by the Japanese throughout Micronesia. Copra exports to Japan and the United States, mainly from the Marshall Islands, continue to this day.

Although economic activity increased as a result of initiatives by outsiders, the Micronesians benefited little from these changes. Only a handful of chiefs and a few foreign companies profited from the copra trade during the early years. The same holds true for most economic activities occurring during the Spanish and German eras. From the colonial governments' point of view, the costs far outweighed the returns between the 1880s and 1914; and, judged by purely commercial standards, the Europeans and their respective governments' outlays were hardly profitable.

Under the Japanese, however, Micronesia attained a measure of self-support in the 1930s and by 1936 generated an annual surplus of one million yen. The sectors mainly responsible for this high level of production were sugar, phosphate fertilizers, copra, and marine resources (mainly dried tuna). All the products were exported to Japan. The following factors played decisive roles in Micronesia's economic management during this period:

1) Land grants, so-called public domain lands, were leased to Japanese companies. 2) Through price supports and tariff benefits, privately owned Japanese commercial enterprises developed close and cooperative relationships with the Japanese government. 3) Subsidies, through direct financial aid, were extended to Japanese farmers and fishermen in the form of start-up capital. 4) By 1940, through unrestricted immigration, 85,000 Japanese nationals were living in Micronesia, compared with only 50,000 Micronesians. 5) Training, technology, and research programs in agriculture and marine resources were provided for the benefit of Japanese commercial undertakings.

The Micronesians derived scant direct benefits from these aggressive development programs, which favored only the Japanese national economy and Japanese enterprises.

Post-War Development

The post-World War II period began with a period of consolidation which has become known as the U.S. Naval Administration phase, 1945 - 1951.

The region was initially designated as one of major importance for U.S. military operations, and access was denied to military forces of other countries. In 1947, de facto exclusive control by the United States was legitimized by the United Nations when it awarded Micronesia (that portion designated as American Micronesia, see Tables 1 and 5) to the United States as a "strategic" Trust Territory.

Under the U.S. Naval Administration, large-scale exploitation of the region's limited resources was terminated with the adoption of two measures: the expulsion of all Japanese citizens and the proscription of large-scale development projects, whether financed by foreign or U.S. private capital. These two policies caused a return to the subsistence economy.

The transfer of political control from the U.S. Navy to the Department of the Interior in 1951 marked the beginning of the second phase of U.S. control. Under civilian rule, the Department of Defense became a tenant of the Trust Territory of the Pacific Islands (American Micronesia). The new civilian administration promoted economic development through an array of governmental programs while discouraging private investment. Stated tenets were respect for Micronesian traditions and the encouragement of self-reliance. U.S. expenditures for the decade of the 1950s were five to six million dollars per annum. Economic development proceeded at a slow pace.

A major change occurred in the early 1960s following Anthony Solomon's report on the political economy of the Trust Territory (1963), and the decision by the Kennedy Administration to Americanize the Micronesians. The shift in policy manifested itself in major investments in social services. Funds for schools and health-care facilities accounted for forty to forty-five percent of the Trust Territory government's budgets during the 1970s, compared with expenditures in these sectors during the 1950s of sixteen to eighteen percent. During the same period, locally hired government personnel increased threefold while salaries paid to Micronesians, in the private as well as in the public sector, increased from $3.3 million in 1961 to $20.5 million in 1970. The subsistence economy was largely augmented by cash salaries, credit, and imports.

After 1970, additional U.S. government assistance was provided through large-scale supplemental funding programs known as Capital Improvement Projects (CIP) and Federal Programs (FP). The CIP funds went for public buildings, airports, paved roads, and other infrastructure projects, while the FP funds financed numerous social programs such as the Civilian Employment Training Agency and U.S. Department of Agriculture surplus-food distribution.

By 1979, 11,000 Micronesians were employed by government agencies in Belau, the Federated States of Micronesia, and the Marshall Islands. The ratio of imports to exports by value ran at an average annual rate of about nine to one. Exports of major commodities such as fish, coconut oil and coconut cake, handicrafts, and returns from tourism reached a high level of $16 million in 1980. (See Figure 20, page 52.) At the same time, imported goods continued to increase. This trend continues today.

In the mid-1980s, economic policies were closely tied to political-status negotiations between the various Micronesian entities and the United States government. These negotiations began in the early 1970s and have resulted in a new relationship termed "free association." The negotiations culminated in the drafting of Compacts of Free Association with three entities: the Federated States of Micronesia (FSM), the Republic of the Marshall Islands, and the Republic of Belau (Palau). As a result, their future economic development is heavily dependent on the economic provisions that are part of these compact agreements. Although there are similarities among the agreements, there also are significant differences of an economic and political nature in the case of each new Micronesian state.

Under the compacts, the governments of the FSM, Belau, and the Marshall Islands will receive basic development grants for fifteen years. In addition, the Marshalls receives special military-impact payments for the U.S. Army missile base at Kwajalein and financial compensation for the effects of radiation from nuclear tests conducted in the Marshall Islands during the 1940s and 1950s.

Other financial arrangements resulting from the compacts include the following:

1. General grants.
These fund current government operations and provide the financial basis for capital improvements. For example, the FSM government will receive a negotiated amount in general grants for the first fifteen years of the compact's duration; over $79 million will be disbursed in the fiscal year 1988, and nearly $37 million for the Marshalls in the same period.

The Republic of Belau was to receive $1 billion over a period of fifty years. The precise terms of that compact agreement are unknown at the time of this writing.

2. Trade preferences.
Trade preferences and exemption from U.S. import duties for each of the Micronesian states are expected to be applied to most manufacturing industries excepting those producing watches, textiles, buttons, footwear, some leather apparel, and tuna packed in oil.

3. Tax advantages.
Resident individuals and American-owned business firms will benefit from tax breaks designed to provide incentives for future growth of the various Micronesian economies.

Whatever the ultimate effects of these arrangements, it is clear that the Micronesians have learned to absorb the various grants and allocations of resources provided by the American government. They have succeeded in integrating the cash economy of the outsiders with the local subsistence economy. For most Micronesians this has involved changes in work values and patterns within the family structure. The changes may be viewed as shifts in utilization of manpower toward a wider participation in the integrated cash/subsistence economies. The future holds, however, an evident dilemma regarding the question of how to lay the economic foundations for greater political independence for the newly emerging island states apart from the United States.

Micronesian Area Fisheries
Marine life, fish, and other marine animals and plants, both coastal and pelagic (oceanic), obviously constitute the foundations of economic growth and development for most of the Micronesian states. Figure 21, page 56, indicates the areal extent (size and distance) of the national seas known as the 200-mile exclusive economic zone (EEZ). In the 1980s, deep-sea ocean fishing continues to be dominated by large foreign fleets, with Japan taking the lead. The individual Micronesian governments have been negotiating fishing agreements with foreigners through licensing arrangements. The resulting license payments, considered as an export, are not adequately or uniformly reported.

The Federated States of Micronesia (FSM), through its government maritime agency, has regularly reported an increase in fees paid by the Japanese, from $2.5 million in 1982 to approximately $4 million in 1986. According to the Executive Director of the FSM Micronesian Maritime Authority, the year-to-year basis of a single-fee payment gave way in late 1984 to a "per-vessel/per-trip" system which determines the actual cost incurred by a single vessel on a single

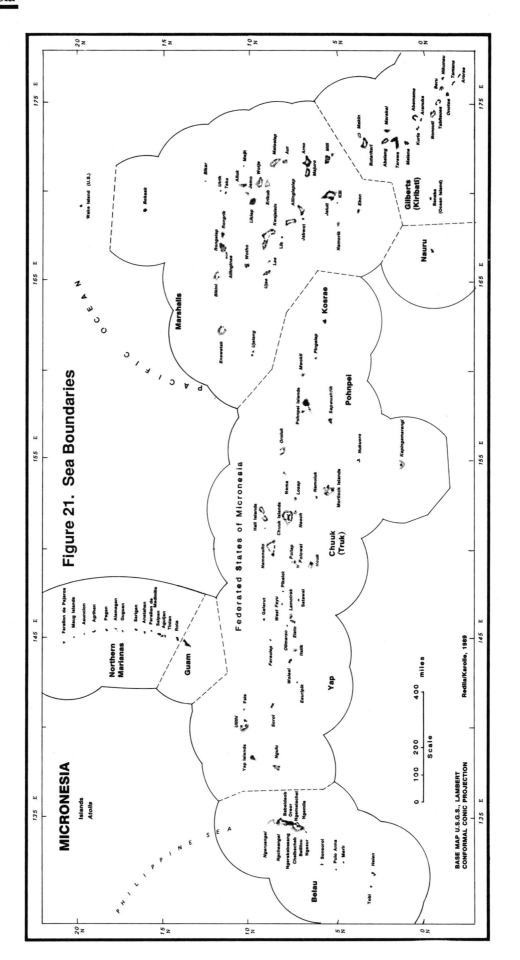

Figure 21. Sea Boundaries

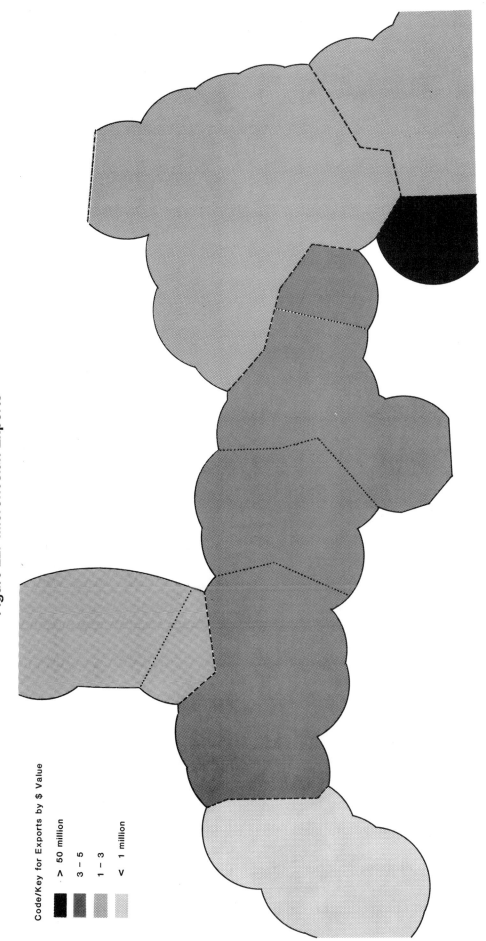

Figure 22. Micronesian Exports

Code/Key for Exports by $ Value

> 50 million

3 – 5

1 – 3

< 1 million

fishing trip within the FSM's EEZ. Additional agreement fees in 1986, especially from the Taiwanese longliners, accounted for about $500,000, thus bringing the total earnings from foreign fishing fleets to about $4.5 million.

The Republics of the Marshall Islands and Palau earned about $1.14 million and $147,000 respectively (Palau's amount decreased from the 1982 level of $385,000). The Republic of Kiribati earned $1.7 million in 1986 from a short-term deal with the Soviet Union. No fisheries data is available from Nauru. The annual average of earnings from the phosphate industry there amounted to over $100 million during the 1970s. The export figure in 1975 was $123 million, decreasing to $75 million in 1979, with imports that year at $11 million. Nauru's 1981 Gross Domestic Product was $155 million; the per-capita income was $21,400.

In the Mariana Islands, both Guam and the Commonwealth of the Northern Mariana Islands (CNMI) indicate fishery income, but both fail to report catch data systematically. For example, both report sizable amounts of tuna trans-shipments (15,000 to 30,000 tons annually during the years 1982 - 84), which represents a combined export earning of nearly $500,000 annually, but exact production figures are lacking.

However, Guam reported small-boat oceanic fisheries of nearly 600,000 pounds caught in 1984, with over 6,000 pounds exported, mainly to Hawaii. Fresh tuna and mahi-mahi amounted to nearly two percent of the estimated Guam catch.

Figure 20 shows the foregoing general economic data by political divisions (six entities: Guam/CNMI, Palau, FSM, Marshalls, Nauru, and Kiribati). The line/shading code indicates the combined value of marine exports and the fishery fees paid to the states of Micronesia.

By nearly all economic and financial indicators available, these newly constituted small island nations presently import many times the value of their exports. While trade turnover is high per capita or per land area, the imbalance of imports over exports, generally, runs ten times higher. For example, Guam's 1983 total value of imported commodities was $636,082,000, while exports in the same year amounted to $39,225,000. This is more than a 13 to 1 ratio of imports over exports by value.

Even at this early stage, there can be no doubt that Micronesians have expectations for continued economic growth. The capital derived from grants and development loans will be expended in full each year by the recipient governments.

Additional expenditures by the United States and other creditor nations will likely be required to keep pace with rapid population growth and increasing demand for material advancement on the part of the Micronesians.

Economic Development: Tourism

The inauguration, in May, 1967, of regular airline service between Guam and Japan set Guam on the road to becoming a major tourist destination. In the ensuing seven years tourist arrivals on Guam increased at an annual rate of nearly 100 percent before leveling off in the mid-1970s at around 200,000 persons annually. A second hotel construction boom beginning in 1977, however, gave renewed impetus to the tourist surge, and in the latter half of the 1980s a total of nearly 600,000 tourists visited the island each year. The steady growth in the number of tourists is thus directly linked with the availability of accommodation and at the present time the boom shows no sign of seriously abating. (See Table 7, page 60.)

There are major concerns, besides the complicated matter of economic dependency. One is that of the large and growing populations in the region and the limited land area at their disposal. What is the optimum population for Guam and for any of the other Micronesian islands? What impact has tourism had on land values? Just how many tourists can be adequately accommodated in these relatively small and fragile tropical environments? And, finally, is the visitor industry indeed the most suitable economic occupation for the islanders?

As the largest number of tourists to the region come from Japan, the Guam tourist industry is naturally dominated by Japanese interests. Since the proportion of tourists from Japan has grown from 20 percent in 1967 to an estimated 88 percent in 1991, this preponderance has become almost total. A comparable trend is evident elsewhere in Micronesia. The proximity of Japan, is, of course, a determining factor in this situation. Figure 1 (page 2) indicates the geographic setting of Micronesia in relation to the neighboring areas of Asia and the Pacific. Figure 2 (page 3) identifies the separate entities and major islands in Micronesia.

The tourist tide is on the rise throughout Micronesia, and there, as in Guam, the overwhelming majority of visitors is Japanese. (See Figures 25 and 26, pages 62 and 63.) This fact underscores the advantage of Micronesia's "rimland" location.

A major factor in the establishment and growth of tourism in Guam and Micronesia has been the islands' physical geography. The tropical climate, dramatic seascapes, and colorful marine life combine to make an attractive environment for visitors, especially those from a highly urbanized, industrialized country such as Japan. The availability of relatively inexpensive air transportation from Japan has also had a stimulating effect. In addition to the lure of Pacific islands for historical, social, and cultural interest, many Japanese visitors are drawn to this American-Micronesian "frontier" by the opportunity to buy duty-free merchandise, as well as by a chance to indulge in a host of vices ranging from prostitution to gambling and drinking. All of these activities and opportunities are important in that they are, in the popular imagination, part of what constitutes a "tropical paradise."

From 1979 to 1983, more than 100,000 tourists visited the Commonwealth of the Northern Marianas (CNMI). Approximately 90 percent of these visitors, mostly from Japan, arrived at and stayed in Saipan. (See Tables 8 and 9, pages 64 and 66.)

Another Micronesian rimland area which receives considerable attention from tourists is Palau (Belau). In the past 10 years an annual average of 5,000 tourists visited the Palau Islands. Palau has an international airport in Irrai (Airai), a few miles from the capital in Koror (Oreor). There are four modern tourist hotels and six smaller rooming houses. A recently built, Japanese-owned and -managed 400-room luxury hotel is in full operation on the island of Ngerekebesang (Arakabesan), less than one mile from Koror.

In the island areas east of the rimlands States of Guam, Palau, and Saipan, CNMI, the tourist industry is clearly less developed. In fact, the numbers of visitors traveling into the Federated States of Micronesia - i.e., Pohnpei and Chuuk (Truk), where most tourists go - show a decrease in the mid-1980s. Annual highs of about 9,000 and 6,000 tourists, respectively, were reached in those two States in 1979-80. Yap State has never developed a visitor industry until very recently, and Kosrae lacked international air links until 1988. However, the potential exists for new and increased development in those islands.

Guam as a Tourist Destination

Guam is the transportation and communication hub of Micronesia. Relatively modern transport infrastructures exist in two locations. (See Figure 24, page 61.) The Guam International Airport provides regular daily and weekly passenger and air-cargo connections to most of the centers in Micronesia, Hawaii, and Southeast and East Asia. Apra Harbor, the center for both military and commercial shipping, is the largest and best-equipped port in the region. Several trans-Pacific communication cables provide the region with telex and video linkages with Southeast Asia, Japan, and, across the Pacific, to North America.

The largest island in Micronesia, Guam is volcanic and comparatively high in elevation. It is situated at the southern end of the Mariana archipelago. In 1990, the population of Guam was conservatively counted at 133,152, unevenly distributed over the island's 554 square kilometers with relatively high density of around 240 persons per km^2. The geographic size and varied topography account for Guam's character and natural beauty. Three distinctive surface divisions are identified: the northern limestone plateau, the dissected volcanic plateau, and the coastal lowlands and associated fringing reefs.

Most tourists enjoy the seascape from a near-ocean hotel, but the coastal plains are limited, narrow, and discontinuous, and lie mainly along the western side of the island. Guam can be divided into three parts: North, Central, and South as shown in Figure 27, page 66.

Most of the major hotels are by Tumon Bay, located on the southern borderland area of the North, and readily accessible from the Central area of the island. (See Figures 27 and 28, pages 66 and 67.) The North and Central regions contain nearly 80 percent of the permanent population. With the large number of tourists in the Tumon Bay area and in the municipality of Tamuning, population densities there are estimated to be double the island average.

Land Ownership

Studies conducted in the mid-1970s indicate that 26.4 percent of all private land was owned by non-residents, including foreign investors. At that time slightly more than 35 percent of all Guam land was controlled by federal authorities, with 33 percent held by the U.S. Navy and Air Force. In addition to military and other federal agency land control, the

Table 7. Visitor Arrivals In Guam According to Purpose of Trip (1967-1989)

Year	Business	Pleasure	Other	Total
1967	99	4,284	117	4,500
1968	725	15,082	2,193	18,000
1969	14,264	30,810	3,191	58,265
1970	10,530	44,580	16,611	73,721
1971	13,325	84,885	20,964	119,174
1972	21,514	139,823	24,052	185,399
1973	25,622	187,471	28,053	241,146
1974	12,460	233,891	4,217	260,568
1975[1]	8,409	128,241	4 0,342	239,695
1976	19,495	105,954	75,895	201,344
1977	31,913	150,118	58,436	240,467
1978	31,075	148,523	52,377	231,975
1979	31,894	173,102	59,330	264,326
1980	33,266	203,784	54,079	291,129
1981	29,897	232,588	50,377	312,862
1982	20,790	241,542	54,414	316,746
1983	19,136	243,122	83,547	345,805
1984	19,260	231,224	110,939	361,423
1985	20,336	236,473	108,129	364,938
1986	21,489	261,703	114,383	397,575
1987	17,462	338,970	121,059	477,491
1988	18,333	472,413	85,424	576,170
1989	18,424	560,007	80,452	658,883

Sources: *Statistical Abstract*, 1976 p. 85.

1985 Guam Annual Economic Review, p. 147

[1]Incomplete reporting year, 1975

1989 Guam Annual Economic Review, p. 165

Government of Guam held another estimated 19-20 percent, much of it unsurveyed. Thus, the private land holdings amounted to about 45 percent of Guam's total, or 250 km² out of 554 km². The pattern of land ownership has shifted in the last 15 years, with both government categories declining slightly, while more privately owned land has been alienated from local residents.

In recent years land purchases by foreign investors have been a major factor in the inflation of land prices. Table 10, page 68, illustrates the land-price spiral in various localities on the island over time. The land most sought after by foreign investors has been in areas suited to the construction of hotels and expensive multi-residential high-rise housing. Coastal and beach-front properties command the highest prices. In the Tumon Bay area, land prices have increased 200-fold in the last 20 years. Recently, for example, beach land sold for nearly $2,000 per km² just to the north of the existing Okura Hotel, and the site of the newly constructed, but not yet open, Nikko Hotel. (See Figure 28.)

Impact on the Economy

While tourism as a service industry opens up employment opportunities for the local people and is a source of revenue for the government, such as, for example, through Guam's hotel room occupancy tax, there remains considerable justification for caution. (See Table 11, page 69.) A business research study by Martin Pray, in the mid-1970s, projected that 160,000 Japanese tourists would come to Guam and that each of those tourists would purchase an average $400 tour package, which would bring in $64 million for the Japanese travel industry. This type of tour includes air fare, hotel charges, and some sightseeing costs, all prepaid to the tour operator in Japan. In the same study the benefit to the Guam economy was calculated by multiplying the number of tourists times their length of stay times their average expenditure per day. The resulting average expenditure per person per day was found to be $130. About sixty percent of this amount was devoted to the purchase of personal items and gifts, with the remaining forty percent going for hotel accommodation, meals, sightseeing, and entertainment. If the 160,000 Japanese tourists projected by the study in 1975 spent $130 per person per day and stayed three nights, they would contribute at least $62 million to Guam's economy in one year. All economic factors indicate that in 1989, utilizing the same methodology and with a daily expenditure of $150 per person, the overall contribution of that year's 600,000 tourists would be over four times the 1974 amount, or some $270 million.

Income from tourism is a significant factor in the economy of Guam and the other islands of Micronesia. When tourists make direct expenditures for a variety of locally produced goods and services, they contribute directly to the level of local self-sufficiency. More than 3,000 persons were engaged in tourism in 1974. By 1985 this number had increased to about 5,500 with an estimated payroll of $68 million in that year. (See Table 12, page 70.)

This tourism income subsequently recirculates in the local economy for purchases of materials and services, wages and salaries of employees, advertising and promotion, taxes, replacement of capital assets, and new construction. Recirculated income from tourism is disbursed throughout the economy, even though a major share of investments in the hotels, tour agencies, and tourist specialty shops is controlled by Japanese entrepreneurs.

For example, in 1984, at least five of the major hotels were Japanese-owned. At that time, they provided 65 percent of the available tourist accommodation. In the same year, there were a total of 2,964 rooms on Guam, which generated $3,501,540 in hotel occupancy tax. In 1988 these figures were 3,939 rooms and tax revenue of $8,825,854. (See Table 11.) Preliminary reports indicate that in 1991, with new hotel construction, room tax revenue will reach nearly $16 million. These figures are expected to increase throughout the 1990s.

Most of the modern tourist hotels on Guam are concentrated in Tumon along the crescent-shaped 3.7 kilometer beach. All major hotels and the smaller hotels are but a short distance from the beach. (See Figures 27 and 28.)

In the early 1980s, there were nine major hotels (Hilton, Pacific Islands Club, Pacific Star, Dai-Ichi, Tropicana, Fujita, Guam Plaza, Reef, and Okura) located on the Tumon Bay beaches and four smaller hotels (Suehiro, Terraza, Joinus, and Tumon Villa). These thirteen hotels represented a capitalization for construction and equipment estimated at $60-100 million. Collectively, the Tumon Bay hotels numbered about 3,000 rooms in 1985.

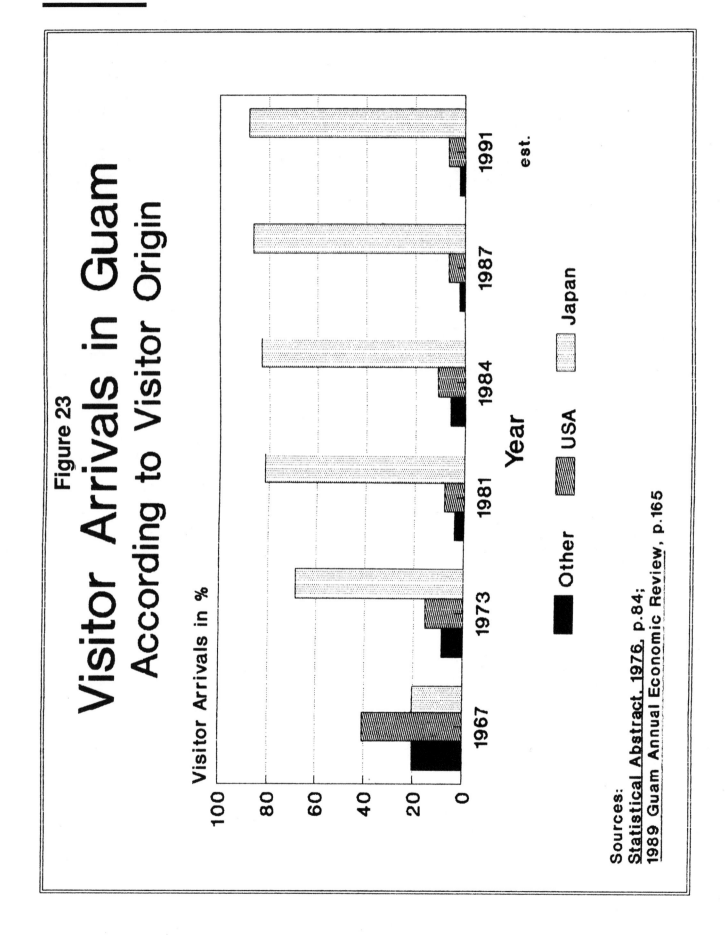

Figure 23

Visitor Arrivals in Guam
According to Visitor Origin

Sources:
Statistical Abstract, 1976, p.84;
1989 Guam Annual Economic Review, p.165

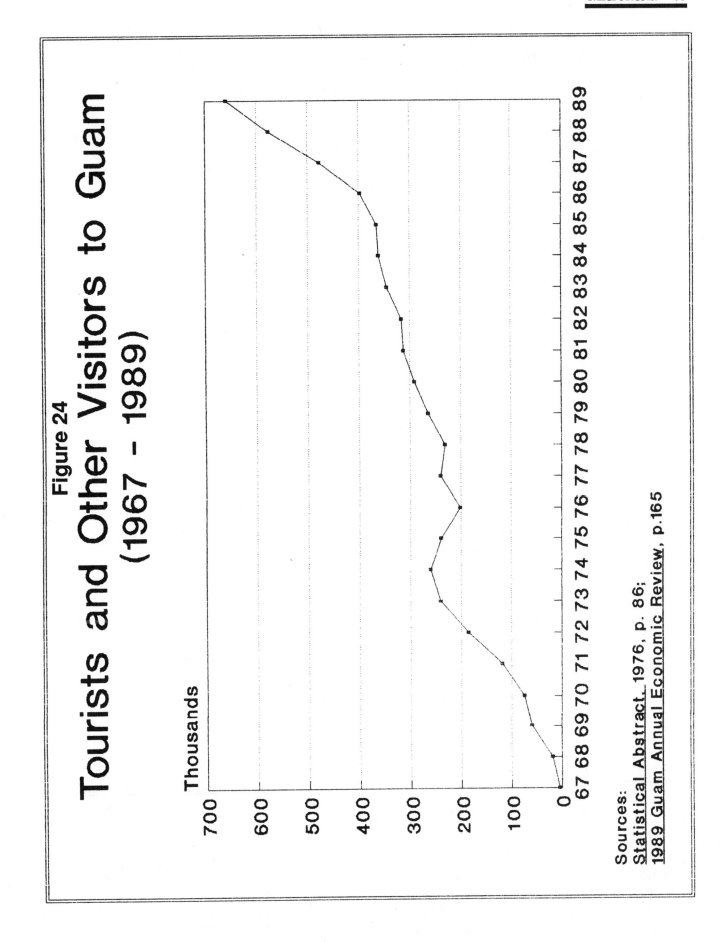

Figure 24

Tourists and Other Visitors to Guam
(1967 – 1989)

Sources:
Statistical Abstract, 1976, p. 86;
1989 Guam Annual Economic Review, p.165

Table 8. Visitor Entries into Micronesia by Country of Origin (1980 and 1984)

Country of Origin	Palau*	Pohnpei	Chuuk	Yap	Northern Marianas
U.S.	2,093 **1,659***	3,374	2,572	748	23,063
%	38 **27***	44	43	55	19
Japan	2,935 **3,195***	2,048	1,496	505	91,205
%	54 **53***	27	25	37	77
Other	410 **1,275***	2,220	1,914	100	5,102
%	8 **20***	29	32	8	4
TOTAL	5,438 **6,129***	7,642	5,982	1,353	119,370

Source: Department of Commerce, *Guam Annual Economic Review*, Agaña, Government of Guam, 1981.

* *1984 Abstract of Statistics*, Palau, 1985.

Six years later, in 1991, the number of Tumon Bay hotels had risen to eighteen, including both the major and smaller hotels. These 18 hotels represent over 4,000 rooms available to the visitors. Figure 6 indicates the major beach hotels with room additions (currently 5 separate hotel expansions) and the sites of eight planned hotels to be built or finished in the near future. The additional eight new hotels will add another 2,000 - 2,500 rooms.

Guam and Micronesia are advantageously placed - even though land sizes are small - in the Western Pacific as bases for future development of the tourist industry. The idea of "small is beautiful" has caught on in a luxury-oriented business endeavor. Rapid development as a major tourist destination, including the construction of relatively large numbers of deluxe hotels and sizable infrastructures, has made tourism an indispensable asset in the island's economy. However, because of the limited land area on Guam as well as in all the other islands, the question arises of what may be the maximum number of people that can be adequately catered to, given the available resources. Inescapable limits to development are bound to reveal themselves in the future.

Table 9. Visitor Entries into Micronesia by State

===

Year	Marshalls	Palau	Pohnpei	Chuuk	Yap	N. Marianas
1971	1,862	2,230	2,428	2,594	2,158	22,337
1972	1,359	2,963	2,749	2,909	1,855	23,488
1973	3,153	4,095	4,079	4,091	1,976	40,905
1974	2,705	3,712	3,702	3,858	1,534	47,434
1975	3,347	5,404	4,632	4,026	1,818	47,413
1976	2,919	4,902	4,215	3,900	1,293	51,739
1977	3,801	5,768	5,904	5,229	1,558	58,103
1978	3,799	4,915	7,004	5,749	1,462	91,373
1979	N/A	5,202	9,295	5,916	926	103,252
1980	N/A	5,438	7,642	5,982	1,353	119,370
1984	2,249	6,129	[FSM total estimate:		10,000]	124,024

Source: Department of Commerce, *Guam Annual Economic Review*,
Agaña, Government of Guam, 1981.

U.S. Department of State, *1984 Annual Report*, Washington, 1985.

In Guam (and even more so in other islands in the region), a large airfield able to accommodate international flights, and modern communications and commercial facilities have helped boost tourist numbers. These swelling numbers and significant acreages of land owned by non-residents point toward future problems. In the private sector the demand for space is acute, as evidenced by the spiraling real estate prices shown in Table 10.

While most reports emphasize the positive aspects of the tourist industry - with the notable exception of Professor Warner, in 1978 - none has measured the economic cost-benefit ratio of tourism on Guam. The most obvious disadvantages are in the areas of environmental degradation, necessary public expenditure for infrastructures, and the single-minded profit orientation of the investors. If the capacity to accommodate tourists is finite, and if the pressure becomes too high for the island's ecosystems, degradation of the environment is inevitable. A cursory examination already suggests that this is indeed the case. Tumon Bay's water quality has declined since 1970, although it is still said to be "adequate" for recreational uses. This adequacy, however, is maintained at the expense of another area, Agaña Bay. The waste water from the sewage treatment plant for the Tumon area is currently discharged over the reef at Agaña Bay, south of the hotel district. The Agaña Bay water is tested regularly by the local water control agency (Environmental Protection Agency) and is often reported in the newspapers as being too polluted for safe swimming or fishing.

The twin aims of preserving the natural environment of Guam and of advancing economic development through tourism are interdependent. The greater the local participation in the tourist industry and the greater the benefits derived by local residents from that industry, the more the local populace will benefit from preservation of the island's physical (and cultural) features, which attract the tourists. If ecological considerations are ignored in poor private and governmental planning, the adverse consequences will be drastic.

Similar trends are discernible in the other

NORTH

Study Area

Guam International
Airport

Commercial Port

CENTRAL

Figure 25
Guam Island

0   1   2 Miles

0 1 2 Kilometers

SOUTH

B. Karolle, 1989

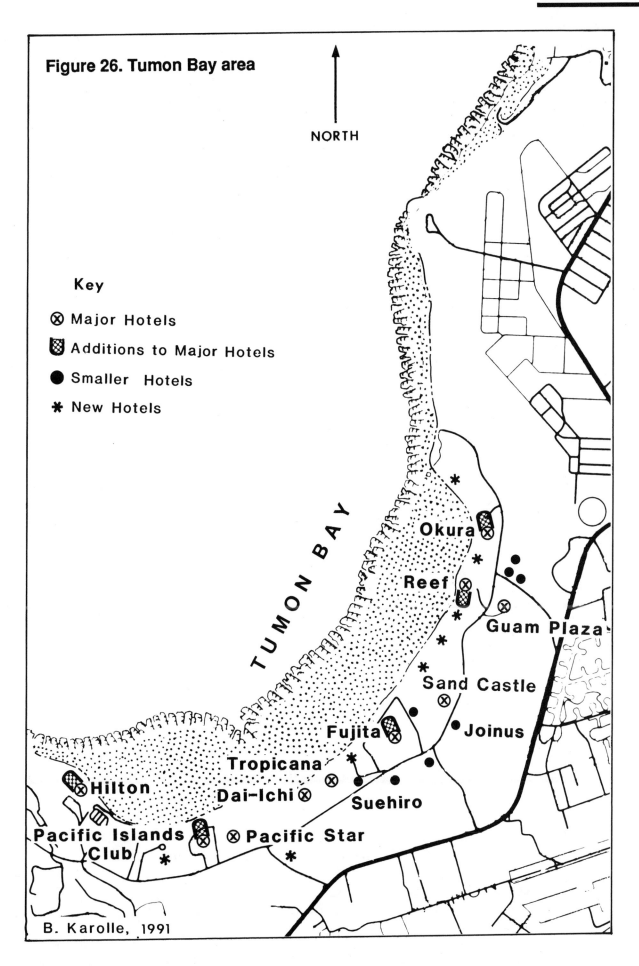

Figure 26. Tumon Bay area

NORTH

Key

⊗ Major Hotels

▨ Additions to Major Hotels

● Smaller Hotels

✳ New Hotels

TUMON BAY

Okura

Reef

Guam Plaza

Sand Castle

Fujita

Joinus

Tropicana

Hilton

Dai-Ichi

Suehiro

Pacific Islands Club

Pacific Star

B. Karolle, 1991

Table 10. Selected Land Values by Site and Classification (1965-1988)

==

a Place/**area**	b Year	c Land type	d* Price per square meter (m²)
North			(US dollars)
1. Dededo	1971	agr/acre	6.75
Dededo	1986	agr/acre	35.00
2. Tumon Bay	1967	beach	10.00
Tumon Bay	1988	beach	672.77
Central			
3. Agaña	1965	res/lot	.77
Agaña	1988	res/lot	44.00
4. Agaña	1965	commercial/ beach>acre	17.65
Agaña	1988	com/beach>acre	150.00
5. Mangilao**	1984	agr/acre	3.51
Mangilao	1988	agr/acre	8.03
South			
6. Inarajan	1970	agr/lot	2.50
Inarajan	1985	agr/lot	6.75
7. Agat	1969	res/lot	7.50
Agat	1983	res/lot	19.60

==

Source: *Compiled by Author, 1989 from Department of Revenue and
Taxation, Government of Guam "appraised value" tax records;
personal interviews with owners.
** Actual purchase price per m².

Table 11. Hotel Occupancy Tax Collection By the Government of Guam and Guam Visitors Bureau Budget

==

Year	Amount Collected (in dollars)	Guam Visitors Bureau Budget (in dollars)
1970	60,200	124,911[2]
1971[1]	188,000[1]	123,441[2]
1972[1]	286,000[1]	117,700[2]
1973[1]	629,500[1]	174,992[2]
1974[1]	700,000[1]	174,992[2]
1975[1]	850,000[1]	277,296
1976	739,412	625,000
1977	817,872	625,000
1978	990,000	725,000
1979	1,354,000	850,986
1980	1,508,000	1,223,506
1981	1,898,000	1,615,803
1982	2,357,000	1,452,906
1983	3,028,000	1,569,674
1984	3,501,540	1,600,802
1985	4,051,467	2,033,807
1986	4,533,912	2,318,706
1987	5,730,243	2,318,706
1988	8,825,854	n/a
1989	10,874,382	n/a
1990	14,250,930	n/a

==

Sources: 1. Hotel Occupancy Taxes, Fiscal Year, Economic Research Center, 1982, p. 118

2. Economic Research Center, 1975, p. 74

3. Guam Visitors Bureau, March 1991, p. 7; and Economic Research Center, 1989, p. 176.

Table 12. Estimated Employment in Tourist-related Enterprises on Guam in 1974 and **1986**

====================================

Type of Enterprise	Number of Employees (1974)	(1986)
Hotels	1,560	**2,300**
Airlines	482	**890**
Tourist shops	422	
Sightseeing companies	139	
Entertainers	100	
Taxis and boats	100	
Car rental agencies	95	
Tour operators	50	
Security companies	40	
Laundries	35	
Government	30	
Travel agencies	30	
Total	3,083	**5,510**

====================================

Sources: Stanford Research Institute (SRI), 1974, p. B-27; and, SRI, **1986**, p. 13, categories of services changed.

island entities of Micronesia, not withstanding the fact that the Federated States of Micronesia and the Republic of the Marshall Islands recently attained nation membership in the United Nations. The expected further growth of the tourist industry in the region as a whole can only exacerbate this drift to deterioration, both in terms of political-economic dependency and in regard to advancing environmental degradation. Unless, of course, the local people can gain control of their respective political economies. Efforts should be made now to limit the damage to the environment and what remains of the indigenous culture, to arrive at a sustainable balance.

Distance Education in Micronesia: The Distance Factor in Terms of Higher Education

Distance Education experiments have been underway in Micronesia using a variety of technological formats since 1985. These experiments, conducted by the University of Guam, respond to the need for year around training directed to the Republic of the Marshall Islands; Kosrae, Pohnpei, Chuuk, and Yap, the four states of the Federated States of Micronesia (FSM); the northern Marianas or the Commonwealth of the Northern Mariana Islands (CNMI); and Palau.

The greatest challenges in delivering training to Micronesia are funding and the various creative methodologies in distance education that must be employed in order to span the 3,000,000 square miles of ocean (more than 7 million square kilometers). This is an area that is roughly equal to that of the continental United States. (See Figures 23 and 24, pages 72 and 73.)

The challenge is further highlighted by the limited availability of technology in each of these developing and culturally diverse island groups. Interactive communications systems are limited to telephone cable, which is commercially accessible and very costly; and the use of single-side band radio, which is licensed through the Federal Communications Commission and limited to medical and educational needs. Recently, the University of Guam has gained authorization to utilize the U.S. GOES satellite under the joint sponsorship of the University of Hawaii's PEACESAT network.

The type of training that has been delivered to Micronesia using distance education formats has been primarily degree credit coursework leading to a bachelor of arts degree in education. There are presently 1,500 students across Micronesia who are enrolled in the University of Guam's Individualized Degree Program (IDP), an advisement and tracking system which allows students continuous enrollment in the program. The IDP system was developed by the UOG College of Education and supported by the UOG Center for Continuing education and Outreach Programs and the various departments of education in each of the jurisdictions. Courses that have been delivered via distance education since 1985 include the following: 1) American History, 2) Counseling Families of Handicapped Children, 3) Ascent of Man, 4) Human Growth and Development, 5) Program Evaluation for Agriculture Extension Agents, 6) Art for Non-Majors, and 7) Internship in Education. There are plans to expand the IDP system to incorporate degree programs in the areas of Business and Nursing, which will have significant implications for the socioeconomic development of Micronesia.

Although distance education delivery has presented challenges to the University, it has proven successful in terms of funding and cost-effectiveness, and in demonstrating the pedagogical soundness of this approach. In addition, the early experiments have resulted in some unexpected cultural findings: 1) distance education has eliminated the concept of the traditional classroom. Students are no longer sitting in front of a instructor listening to a lecture; they are reading independently (guided by the instructor) and viewing videotapes, which allows the option for continuous, student-initiated repetition of content. The various languages in each of the Micronesian islands differs, and this option proved most helpful in understanding and synthesizing information within course content that is provided in English. 2) During radio interactive sessions, which were typically one hour and 30 minutes long each week, Micronesian students tended to ask more content specific questions, a behavior that is not always observed in traditional classrooms since many Micronesian students are reluctant to participate in discussions and are more inclined to give the floor to native English language speakers. 3) There was more informal, student-initiated discussion among class peers on content, and, 4) the most significant finding in distance education experiments in Micronesia proved to be the willingness of the students to question the cultural relevancy of course content to their unique socio-economic environment; for example, during the Internship in Education course, students questioned various classroom strategies in managing children with behavior problems within the context of child rearing patterns of their culture. This allowed immediate feedback, modified application of content and more effective teaching.

The distance education formats that have proved successful in Micronesia include the use of commercially produced videotape series; use of single-side band radio for sessions between students and instructors; and use of the mail system and facsimile transmission for the exchange of printed material. With the installation of satellite dishes at the University of Guam, the option to utilize computer-assisted instruction (CAI) and computer interactive sessions via the U.S. GOES satellite will open up additional opportunities to provide training to those isolated island groups.

As the technology in communications and computer accessibility increases and becomes more available in Micronesia, particularly in the area of international library access, the sophistication of distance education training will be enhanced, bringing further opportunities for more relevant training and advanced research on the cultural, political, economic, and social systems of Micronesia.

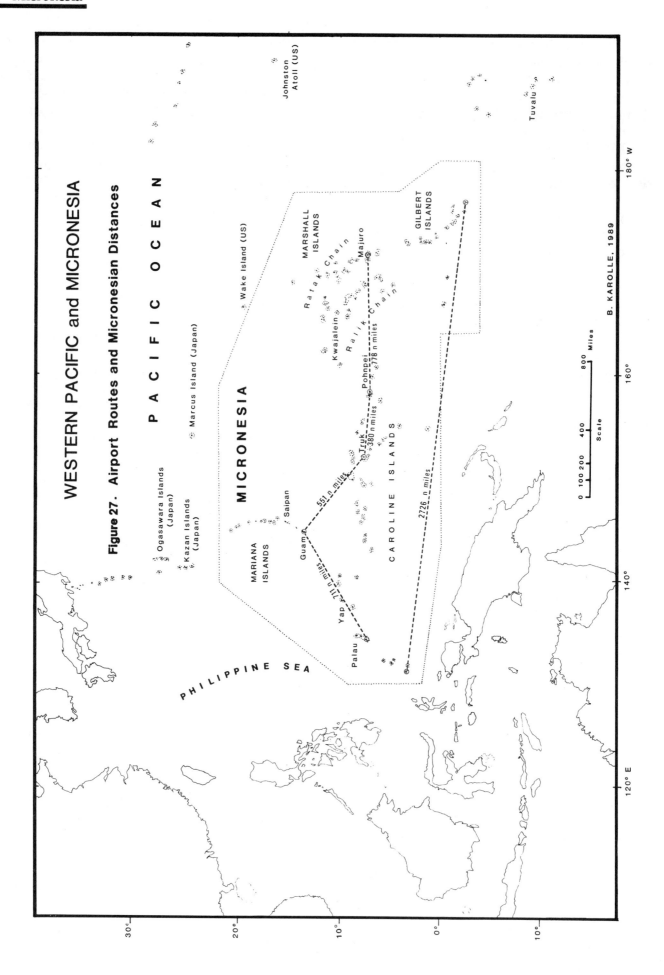

WESTERN PACIFIC and MICRONESIA

Figure 27. Airport Routes and Micronesian Distances

B. KAROLLE, 1989

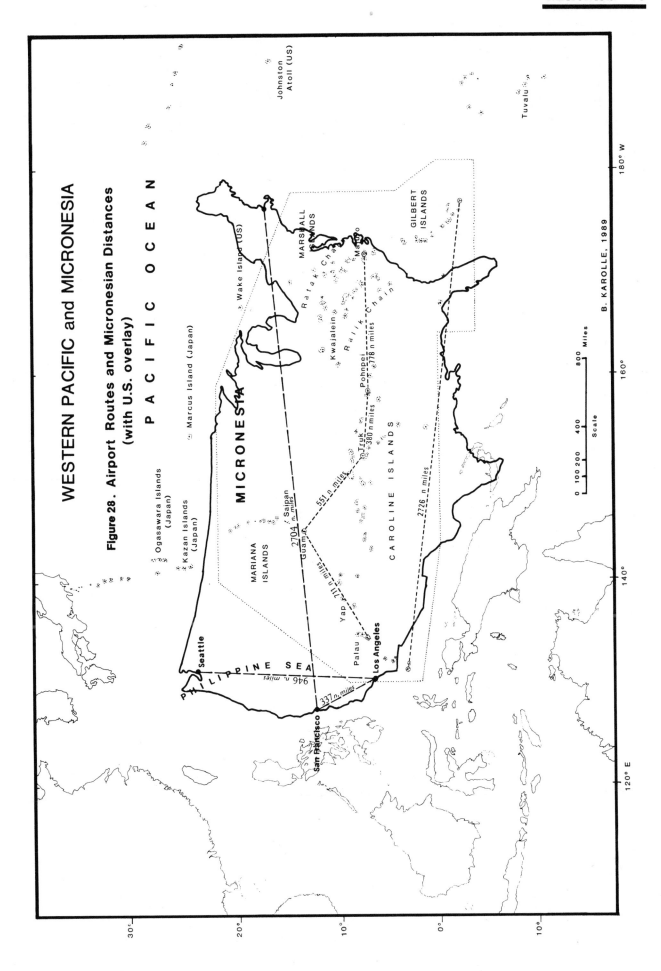

WESTERN PACIFIC and MICRONESIA

Figure 28. Airport Routes and Micronesian Distances
(with U.S. overlay)

P A C I F I C   O C E A N

Johnston
Atoll (US)

Tuvalu

180° W

Wake Island (US)

Marcus Island (Japan)

MARSHALL
ISLANDS

GILBERT
ISLANDS

R a t a k   C h a i n

Majuro

R a l i k   C h a i n

Kwajalein

Pohnpei

778 n. miles

MICRONESIA

Truk
380 n. miles

551 n. miles

2226 n. miles

B. KAROLLE, 1989

160°

800 Miles

0 100 200   400

Scale

Ogasawara Islands
(Japan)

Kazan Islands
(Japan)

Saipan

2704 n. miles

Guam

Yap
711 n. miles

MARIANA
ISLANDS

Palau

CAROLINE ISLANDS

Los Angeles

140°

Seattle

P H I L I P P I N E   S E A

946 n. miles

337 n. miles

San Francisco

120° E

30°

20°

10°

0°

10°

Climate and Weather

The Inter-tropical Convergence zone (ITC) is a climate belt encircling the earth and centered near the equator. This zone is produced by the convergence of the northeast and southeast trade winds (NE and SE Trades) and is characterized by ascending, warm moist air, westward-tracking low-pressure air masses, variable winds and calms, numerous cumulus clouds, and squalls. At sea the ITC may expand into broad areas known as doldrums. The ascending air of the ITC circles at high altitudes toward the poles. In the neighborhood of latitudes 30 degrees north and south, it descends and contributes to the formation of the subtropical high-pressure zones of the horse latitudes (30 - 35 degrees N. & S. latitude) and on land the major deserts of the world. Subsequently, this air circles back toward the equator, to converge, rise, and repeat the cycle. In the northern hemisphere, the air moving southward toward the equator is deflected by the eastward rotation of the earth, the Coriolis effect, to become the NE Trades. In the southern hemisphere, the SE Trades are similarly produced. (See Figure 29, below.)

These low-altitude atmospheric zones, i.e., ITC and trade winds, are disturbed by land masses, but they are well developed across oceans. In the western portion of the tropical North Pacific, the general area of Micronesia, the ITC intensifies north of the equator with the northern hemisphere summer and diminishes with the southern hemisphere summer. The NE Trades move northward and weaken as the ITC intensifies and moves toward the equator and strengthens with the diminishing of the ITC. This produces an important annual reversal of doldrums and trade winds for much of Micronesia.

Because temperature fluctuates little in the tropics, especially near sea level and at insular locations, the important climatic factors in Micronesia are rainfall and wind. Graphs illustrating these two parameters for eight major weather stations, those with comprehensive and long-term data over 28 to 39 years, are placed in nearly relative positions on a map of Micronesia in Figure 30, page 76. Data for Tarawa, in the Gilbert Islands (Kiribati), are from the New Zealand Meteorological Service (1984). The remaining seven stations are all from the major United States National Oceanic and Atmospheric Administration (U.S. NOAA, 1984a.) weather stations in Micronesia: Guam in the Mariana Islands, Oreor (Koror), Yap, Truk, Pohnpei (Ponape) in the Caroline Islands, and Kwajalein and Majuro in the Marshall Islands.

Figure 29. Atmospheric Circulation Near the Equator

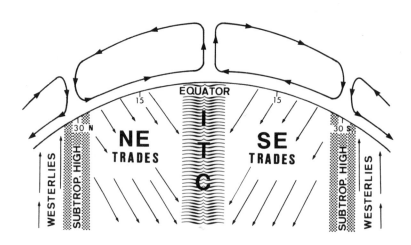

R. KRIZMAN, 1987

Rainfall

Ronald C. Taylor's published isohyet (lines of equal rainfall) estimates are of mean monthly and annual rainfall for the tropical portion of the Pacific Ocean. His illustrations were based on data obtained from 118 island stations, over 40 in the Micronesian area. Figure 31, page 77, is a portion of Taylor's illustration of mean annual isohyets. The distinctive feature is the pattern of concentric isohyets centered over the eastern Caroline Islands. From this high (200 inches of rainfall - yearly average), rainfall generally decreases in all directions. The rate of decrease is most rapid to the north and northeast and less steep in other directions. The decrease toward the Gilbert Islands deepens, broadens, and extends south of the equator to the coast of South America.

Taylor's monthly isohyets show similar highs enclosing the Carolines for the entire year. In mid-year and especially September this high moves northward about five degrees of latitude, expands, and thus includes the lower Mariana Islands. During the remainder of the year, the area of high rainfall contracts to its original location. This is a reflection of the annual movement and enhancement of the ITC.

Figure 32, page 77, compares annual rainfall for the eight major stations in Micronesia. Means are indicated by the horizontal lines; the recorded range, by the full extent of the vertical line; and the 95 percent confidence interval (+ -2 standard deviations), by the vertical block. All stations record generous mean annual rainfall. The highest is registered at Pohnpei: an annual mean of 190 in., a 38-year maximum of 236 in., measurable rain occurring 300 days per year, and all months normally receiving in excess of ten inches. Rainfall is lowest and most variable in the Gilbert Islands, where Tarawa reports an annual mean of 78 in., a 39-year minimum of 16 in., rain spread over 144 days per year, and all months having near zero precipitation. The confidence interval is the computed range in which 95 percent of all future total annual rainfalls will occur if a normal frequency distribution is assumed. The assumption of a normal distribution is highly suspect. See Table 13, page 78, for station mean and extremes. Data for Honolulu, Hawaii, is included for comparison. None of the stations has reported individual years with twice their mean annual rainfall. Tarawa approached this with 175 percent of normal followed by Guam with 164

percent. Only Tarawa has had years with less than half of its normal rainfall. This occurs at an average of once every eight years, with 20 percent of normal being the extreme. Kwajalein follows with a year of 58 percent of normal. Annual rainfall at Tarawa is by far the most variable year to year. Its computed coefficient of variation (v = 100 S.D. / x⁻) is 41. Guam and Kwajalein follow with 23 and 20 respectively. The remaining stations - Majuro, Yap, Truk, Oreor, and Pohnpei - decrease from 15 to 11. These stations, Majuro, Yap, Truk, Oreor, and Pohnpei, have the most consistent mean annual rainfalls.

Rare but severe droughts of short duration do occur. During the first five months of 1983, the Marshalls and the extreme eastern Caroline Islands received only about 13 percent of their normal rainfall, and the Marianas and western Carolines about 28 percent. Drastically reduced rainfall had devastating effects on stream flow, water catchment, and agriculture. Rainfalls for the entire year of 1983 were the lowest of record in 30 years for Majuro, Pohnpei, and Yap and averaged 70 percent of normal. Other Micronesian stations received an average of 77 percent of normal. Tarawa was apparently not affected. This drought was broad in area and was attributed by Otto van der Brug of the United States Geological Survey to the El Niño effect. Normally, the trade winds drive the eastern Pacific Ocean surface currents to the west and cause an upwelling of deep cold water and nutrients along the west coast of the Americas. A lessening of the trade winds and their replacement by westerly winds produces the El Niño; warm seawater flows abnormally to the west coast of the Americas, thus preventing the normal upwelling and subsequent nourishment of fishes. The El Niño of 1983 was possibly the strongest in 100 years.

The distribution of rainfall within the average year (see Figure 30) produces wet and dry periods or what actually are, for the most part, very- and less-wet periods. Based upon a ratio computed by dividing total mean rainfall occurring during the driest consecutive four months by the total mean rainfall of the wettest four months, it was determined that Guam (with a ratio of 36) displayed the most distinct wet-dry periods: on the average a quantity equal to 36 percent of the wet-period rain falls in the dry period. Next less distinct periods are found on Kwajalein, Tarawa, and Yap (43-47), followed by Oreor, Truk, and

Figure 30. Cyclone Tracts and Monthly Distribution of Rainfall and Wind for Stations in Micronesia

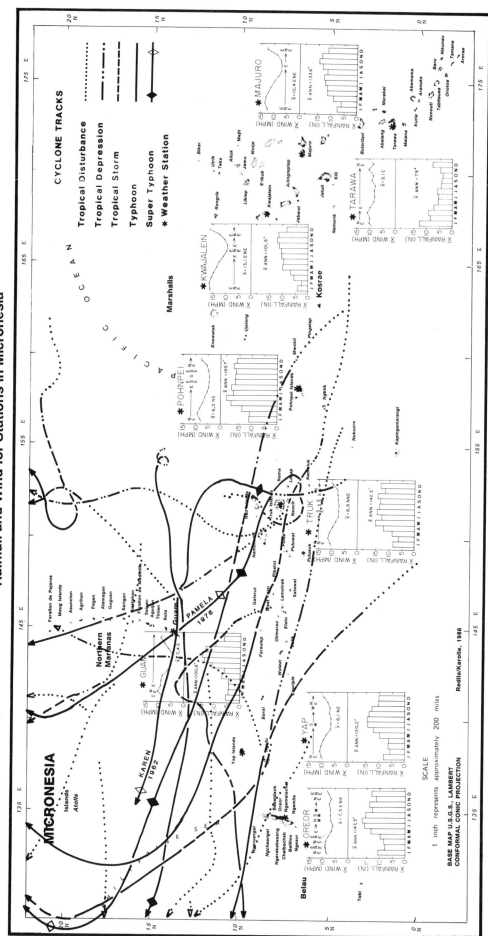

Figure 31. Isohyets of Total Annual Rainfall

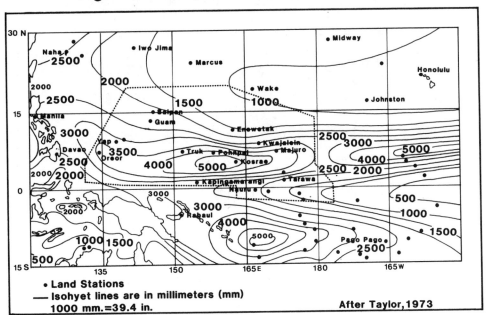

Figure 32. Annual Rainfall for Stations in Micronesia

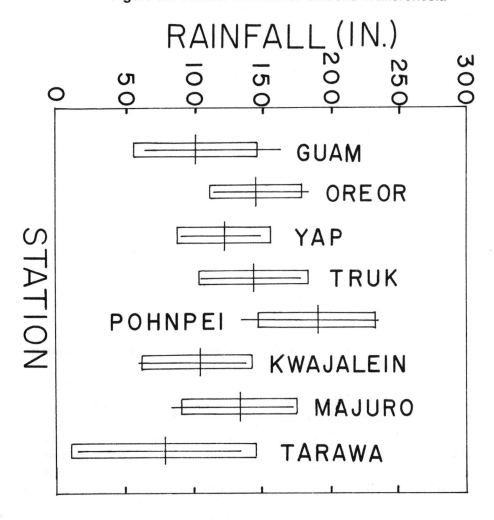

Table 13. Annual Rainfall, Station Means, and Extremes (Inches)

==

Station	Mean Annual	Lowest (Year)	Highest (Year)
Guam	100.8	66.9 (73)	165.9 (76)
Oreor	147.3	114.6 (70)	185.0 (74)
Yap	120.2	88.4 (83)	149.1 (62)
Truk	142.3	104.4 (82)	179.2 (62)
Pohnpei	189.7	133.6 (83)	236.3 (76)
Kwajalein	101.5	59.4 (84)	139.4 (64)
Majuro	133.6	86.3 (83)	173.1 (56)
Tarawa	71.0	15.6 (50)	136.0 (72)
Mean/ Extremes	126.7 /	15.6	236.3
Honolulu, Hawaii*	22.7	5.0 (83)	42.8 (65)

==

Source: Tarawa - New Zealand Meteorological Service, 1984; other stations - U.S. NOAA, 1984a.

* Included for comparison.

Majuro (60-65), and, finally, Pohnpei (70), which had the least distinct wet-dry periods. The driest four-month period occurs on Tarawa (16.5 in.), followed by Guam and Kwajalein (about 19 in.). Truk and even Pohnpei do have short periods - two or three months - of reduced rainfall.

There is a general consistency among all stations, except Tarawa, in that February is the month of least rainfall. That month is followed by January, March, and then April. The February mean for Kwajalein at 2.7 inches is the lowest of all monthly means. With more variability, the months of most rainfall extend from July through October. The annual pattern for Tarawa is a near reversal of the one stated above. No station except Kosrae demonstrates a bimodal curve of rainfall, with a

major high in April and a secondary high in December.

Typically, rain in Micronesia is brief but intense. It extends over a limited area and falls from scattered cumulus clouds. These are convectional or convergent rains, occurring where a parcel of warm moist air rises, cools beyond its dewpoint temperature, forms clouds, and releases rain. Rains of this type are most frequent in mid-year, when the ITC is northward. At this time easterly waves also become an important source of rain. These waves are elongated zones of low pressure, oriented perpendicular to the trade winds, and moving with them. Their passage is accompanied by squall activity. Prolonged, heavy rains from completely cloudy skies are generally

Table 14. Mean Annual Rainfall of Lesser Stations in
Micronesia and Stations in the Adjacent Areas*

===

Station	Inches	Station	Inches
Enewetak	57.9	Marcus	43.4
Nauru	81.1	Midway	43.3
Saipan	81.0	Iwo Jima	52.8
Kapingamarangi	110.6	Davao	77.6
Kosrae	200.6	Manila	82.0
		Naha	82.8

Johnston	27.0	Rabaul	88.8
Wake	36.4	Pago Pago	123.8

===

Source: Van der Brug, 1984b, 1985; U.S. Dept. of Commerce, 1969;
U.S. NOAA, 1984a & b; Taylor, 1973.

* All stations are located on map, Figure 31.

brought by large cyclonic storms, which are again more common in mid-year. Lightning/thunder storms might occur nearly weekly during the months of high rainfall, but they are otherwise uncommon. In the early months of the year, during the dry season, weak fronts press down from the north, bringing shear lines and storms especially to the northern portion of Micronesia. Prolonged light rains, common in some temperate climates, are unusual in Micronesia. On an annual basis, the sun shines in Micronesia about 54 percent of daylight time; Tarawa has the high average of 60 percent, while Pohnpei averages a low 43 percent. Overall, almost 80 percent of days are considered cloudy, almost 20 percent partly cloudy, and only about 2 percent are clear.

James C. Sadler summarized two years of satellite cloud observations of a global strip between latitudes 30 north and south. Constant features of the monthly figures for the central and western Pacific are: a band of cloudiness north of the equator (reflective of the ITC), areas of reduced cloudiness indicating the trade wind fields, and very heavy cloudiness extending through Borneo, New Guinea, and the Solomons. Considerable variation between the two years observed tends to mask more detailed features.

It is acknowledged that high islands - all major weather stations except Kwajalein, Majuro, and Tarawa - intercept more rain than do atolls; and that rainfall is locally more variable on high islands. On Guam, the official (NOAA weather station, located in the northern portion of the island) annual mean is 100.8 in., while Naval Air Station in central Guam averages 87.4 in. Totals of over 110 in. may occur in the southern mountains and on the windward northeast portions of the northern plateau. A minimum of about 80 in. annually falls on the leeward west coast of central Guam. Recently, J. F. Mandy provided an updated mean annual rainfall map for Guam. Rainfall in the interior mountains of Pohnpei and Kosrae is estimated to reach 400 in. Table 14, above, provides selected mean annual rainfall data from lesser stations in Micronesia and from stations in the adjacent areas. (See Figure 31.)

Wind
The northeast trade winds (NE Trades) predominate in Micronesia. The team of Klaus

Wyrtki and G. Meyers studied the trade wind field over the Pacific Ocean by analyzing some five million shipboard observations, taken mostly as Beaufort estimates (wind scale measurements). About one-half million of these observations were in the Micronesian area. These data were sorted by quadrangles of two degrees latitude by ten degrees longitude and averaged for various time periods including monthly and annually. Over the Pacific in general, the NE Trades are strongest during November through May, with maximum expansion in April. They are weakest during June to October, with least expansion in September.

The portion of Wyrtki and Meyers's monthly illustrations which displays apparent maximum and minimum expansion of the NE Trades into Micronesia in February and September respectively is included as Figure 24. The February portion shows strong (length of arrows indicates miles per hour) NE Trades throughout all of Micronesia, especially the central area, where the westerlies have moved to below 30 degrees north latitude and an area of doldrums exists east of New Guinea. During the ensuing months, the area of doldrums migrates to the northwest so that by September it lies in south-central Micronesia. The September figure shows four additional features: a weakened NE Trades with a more easterly origin, influence from the Asian summer (southwest) monsoon into the western Carolines, the SE Trades affecting the Gilberts, and a sharp line of convergence between the NE and SE Trades which extends eastward at about eight degrees north latitude. This line of convergence (ITC) is a constant feature of the central Pacific and wavers annually between about 3 and 15 degrees north latitude.

Winds recorded at island stations correlate well with the shipboard observations. Of the eight major stations, Kwajalein displays the strongest winds, generally 10 to 15 miles per hour and from the east-northeast. Those on Majuro are slightly reduced. The remainder of the stations are less affected by the trade winds and record mean winds, which fluctuate between 5 and 10 MPH. The official wind speeds at Pohnpei are the lowest, but this is undoubtedly due to the protected location of the weather station. Oreor has the flattest annual curve, the most varied directions, and probably the lowest actual speeds. (See Figure 30.)

During the post mid-year period, there is a correlation in most of Micronesia between the reduction of the NE Trades, the northward intensification of the doldrums, and increased rainfall. During the last and especially the first several months of the year, there is a reverse correlation between an expanded NE Trades, a southward shift of the doldrums, and reduced rainfall. Tarawa presents the exception to this pattern. During the middle of the year, Tarawa is affected by the dry SE Trades and during the rest of the year by the NE Trades.

The trade winds cause large waves in the ocean, while during the doldrum period the surf is gentle except when heightened by storms. Winds, like rainfall, can be locally modified by topography, especially on the largest and highest islands. Winds are more pronounced on the windward sides of islands, usually northeast, and in high, open locations. Even with strong winds at such sites, it can be completely calm behind rises, in depressions, or in forests. During windless periods, high islands may demonstrate gentle diurnal up- and end down-slope breezes. Staying out of the sun and being exposed to moving air considerably increases human comfort in the tropics.

Typhoons

Large and sustained low-pressure systems tend to develop more frequently in Micronesia in the post-mid-year period when the ITC has intensified northward. Occasionally these tropical disturbances develop into cyclones. These are closed systems circulating counterclockwise (clockwise in the southern hemisphere) around an area of extremely low pressure. The calm central area - the eye - can be more than twenty miles in diameter and is often completely surrounded by a wall cloud. Beyond the wall are stormy areas of high winds and rains. These areas may spread to a diameter of 300 miles or more.

The winds around and within a cyclone usually intensify as the storm moves. Movement is generally to the west or northwest. Successive stages of intensification are recognized by the maximum speed of sustained surface winds. Stages are named: tropical depression (TD), winds of 33 knots or less; tropical storm (TS), 34-63 kts.; typhoon (TY), 64-129 kts. (east of 180 degrees typhoons are called hurricanes); and super-typhoon (STY), 130 kts. or greater. (See appendix A for conversion of knots to MPH.)

Figure 33. Mean Surface Wind Velocities for February and September

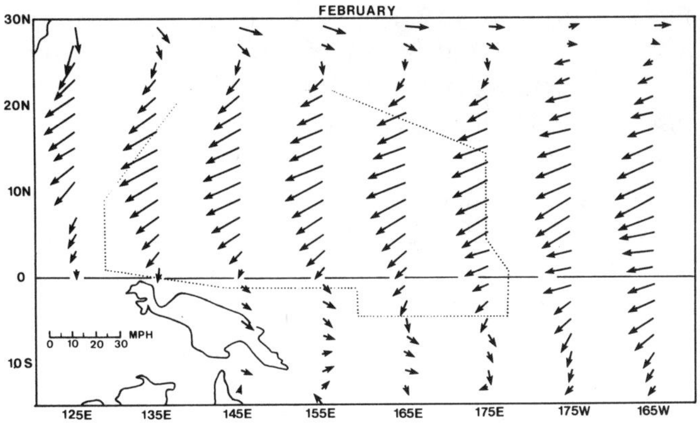

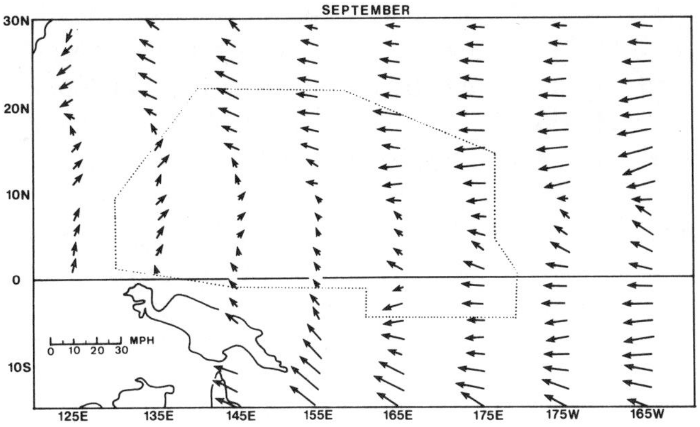

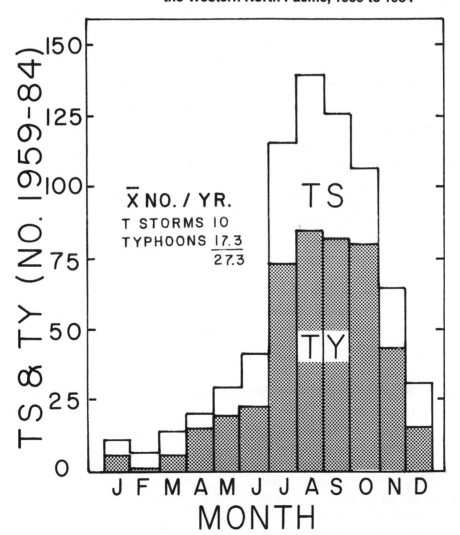

After Wyrtki and Meyers, 1975

Figure 34. Monthly Distribution of the Total Numbers of Tropical Storms and Typhoons Occurring in the Western North Pacific, 1959 to 1984

Between 1959 and 1984, a mean of 17 typhoons (including supertyphoons) and ten tropical storms per year were observed and recorded in the western North Pacific. This area extends from 180 degrees longitude to the Asian mainland and normally accounts for about 40 percent of such storms in the entire world. A monthly distribution of the total numbers of western Pacific storms occurring in this 26-year period is shown graphically in Figure 34, page 81. It is immediately apparent that although they may occur during any month of the year, there is a definite storm season, which begins abruptly in July and diminishes in November. This five-month period, which corresponds with the northward intensification of the ITC, accounts for 75 percent of these storms.

In 1984, the number of cyclones occurring in the western North Pacific approached mean numbers. Two-thirds of these storms had origins in the broad Micronesian areas. The approximate tracks of these storms are included in Figure 30. The strongest stages of intensification reached by these storms while still in Micronesia were 2 STY, 6 TY, 3 TS, 4 TD, and six that never developed above the tropical disturbance level until after leaving the area. During 1984, nearly half of all western Pacific cyclones, especially those occurring later in the year, followed the classic pattern of recurving to the northeast and dissipating harmlessly over cooler waters. Most of the remainder struck the Asian coastal islands or the Asian mainland anywhere from Vietnam to northern Japan. In 1985, few storms recurved while still over open water and those which did tended to be earlier in the year.

Also included in Figure 30 are the tracks of supertyphoons Karen, November 1962, and Pamela, May 1976. These were the two most severe storms to hit Guam in modern history. Both storms passed directly over Guam and resulted in extensive damage to buildings, utilities, crops, and natural vegetation. Thirteen deaths on Guam were attributed to Karen and miraculously only one to Pamela. The dollar value of the destruction on Guam resulting from Pamela alone was estimated at $300 million. Karen struck Guam with sustained winds of 150 kts., had gusts of 180 kts., traveled rapidly at 17 kts., and was dry, releasing only eight inches of rain. Pamela delivered sustained winds of 120 kts., gusts of 145 kts., moved at only seven kts., and drenched the island with about 30 inches of rain. As a storm passes, winds may come from various directions depending on the position of the storm.

Typhoon-strength cyclones are uncommon near Yap and are rare in Belau and in the Marshalls. In the late 1950s two storms struck Pohnpei within two months of each other. The next major storm struck nearly thirty years later, in May 1986. Numerous storms form in the area of Truk, but few achieve damaging intensity until moving westward. Guam is struck on an average of every two years by cyclones containing 50 kts. or stronger winds, every three and one-half years by 64 kts. or stronger winds, and about every ten years by storms approaching supertyphoon strength.

Temperature

Mean annual air temperatures for the official stations in Micronesia vary from a low of 78.8 degrees Fahrenheit (F) on Guam to a high of 82.8 degrees F on Tarawa. See Table 15, page 83, for station means, range, and extremes. (Honolulu is included for comparison.) The extreme air temperatures reported from the eight stations are a minimum of 54 degrees F on Guam and a maximum of 97 degrees F on Yap and Kwajalein. The range of temperatures between the coolest and warmest months of the year is very slight, averaging only 1.2 degrees F. This range is considerably narrower than the mean range of daily temperatures, 11.1 degrees F. Compared with the temperatures found at higher latitudes these temperatures and ranges are extremely mild.

Low monthly means typically occur in the first two or three months of the year, during the drier and more windy periods, and contribute to more comfortable climatic conditions in the first quarter. Only on Truk and Pohnpei do low monthly means occur in mid-year. High means are seen during any of the remaining months but are more common in May or September. Variations in air temperature reflecting micro-climate situations are subtle in Micronesia. The local lapse rate is two or three degrees F per 1,000 feet of elevation; draining and pooling of cool air is weak and occurs only during windless periods. Nocturnal temperatures occasionally decrease beyond dewpoint, thus resulting in the formation of dew.

The warm and constant air temperatures in Micronesia are due to the area's equatorial location, the stabilizing effect of extensive ocean areas, high atmospheric humidity, and warm

Table 15. Temperature, Station Means, Ranges, and Extremes (Degrees F)

Station*	Annual Mean	Range Between Lowest & Highest Monthly Mean	Mean Annual Daily Maximum	Mean Annual Daily Minimum	Highest Maximum Recorded	Lowest Minimum Recorded
Guam	78.8	2.8	85.3	72.2	95	54
Oreor	81.5	1.4	87.6	75.5	95	69
Yap	81.0	1.4	86.8	75.2	97	65
Truk	81.3	0.4	86.4	76.2	94	66
Pohnpei	80.6	0.9	87.1	74.1	96	66
Kwajalein	81.7	0.9	86.5	77.0	97	68
Majuro	81.0	0.6	85.4	76.6	91	69
Tarawa	82.8	0.9	88	77.5	95.5	68
Means/ Extremes	81.1	1.2	86.6	75.5 /	97	54
Honolulu, Hawaii**	77.0	8.4	84.2	69.7	94	53

Source: Tarawa - New Zealand Meteorological Service, 1984; other stations - U.S. NOAA, 1984a.

* Stations record daily maximum and minimum temperatures; all means and ranges are derived from these readings.

** Included for comparison.

ocean currents. The equatorial location assures constant and intense insolation (direct solar radiation) throughout the year. This stabilizes both air and sea temperatures. Water, having a high specific heat (being very slow to absorb and release heat), further moderates fluctuations in air temperatures. Constantly high humidity adds to the stabilization of air temperatures, and thus water vapors absorb heat and act as an insulative blanket which retards the absorption of radiation by the earth's surface.

Ocean Temperatures

Warm ocean currents that hover near mean annual air temperatures add to the stabilization of air temperatures. At the northern edge of Micronesia, between 15 degrees and 20 degrees north latitude, the mean sea surface temperature is 82 degrees F with an annual range of six degrees. Since sea temperatures only gradually increase, their range decreases until five degrees north and south of the equator, where surface temperatures are 83 degrees F with an annual range of only one degree.

Humidity

Due to generous rainfall and warm oceans and air, Micronesia has constantly high humidity. (See Table 7 for station means. Honolulu is again

Table 16. Relative Humidity, Station Means (percent)

Station*	Annual Mid-day x-	High Monthly Mid-day x- (mo.)	Low Monthly Mid-day x- (mo.)	High Monthly Nocturnal x- (mo.)
Guam	76	81 (11)	72 (4,5)	96 (8,9)
Oreor	77	78 (6-8)	74 (3,4)	93 (6)
Yap	77	79 (9,10)	73 (3)	92 (7,10)
Truk	77	79 (5,6,12)	75 (2,3)	90 (7,8)
Pohnpei	78	79 (5-7)	76 (1-3)	96 (8,9)
Kwajalein	75	77 (5-8)	69 (2)	85 (5,7)
Majuro	76	78 (5,6)	73 (2)	85 (5)
Means (x)	77	73	79	91
Honolulu, Hawaii**	56	52 (7,9)	63 (1)	82 (1)

Source: U.S. NOAA, 1984a.

* Stations report humidity four times a day, at six-hour intervals; exact schedules may vary between stations.

** Included for comparison.

included for comparison.) Annual mid-day means at all stations (except Tarawa, where data are not available) average 77 percent. Stations determine relative humidity at six-hour intervals, but various exact times are utilized. In this discussion, "mid-day" data are those taken once daily at each station sometime between eleven in the morning and four in the afternoon. The month of high mid-day humidity, at a mean of 79 percent, is typically the month of high rainfall, May through December, depending upon the station. The month of low mid-day humidity, at 73 percent, is during low rainfall, January through May. This moderate drop is sufficient to increase human comfort. Minimum extremes at less than 65 percent are seldom recorded. High daily humidity predictably occurs during the coolest time of the day, between three and six in the morning. High monthly nocturnal mean humidity averages 91 percent.

Summary

The general climate of Micronesia is characterized by warm to hot air temperatures which fluctuate very little annually and only moderately on a daily basis. Rainfall and humidity are high year-round and increase near mid-year with the northward intensification of the Inter-tropical Convergence zone (ITC). Winds are light and variable in direction at mid-year. During the first months of the year, the ITC zone diminishes. At this time rainfall and humidity decrease, and the northeast trade winds (NE Trades) bring relief from the normally sultry tropical climate. Tropical cyclones commonly form in the central Caroline Islands and achieve damaging strength by the time they move westward to the Marianas.

PART 3 - INDIVIDUAL ISLANDS AND ATOLLS

Introduction

In this section, nine of the designated 123 island units appear. (Refer to Table 2, page 3, and Figure 12, page 28.) While these particular selections represent a relatively small number of the total islands, they provide the reader with an introduction to a key set of individual and varied Micronesian communities throughout the region. Rather than suggesting that the nine represent typical Micronesian islands, it would be more accurate to describe them as representative and vital to their respective areas and their overall significance within the region.

Every attempt has been made to provide an integrated areal examination of each place. The qualitative maps of this section express the main social, economic, and physical characteristics of each island.

Particular cartographic attention has been given to several spatially important features of these islands: characteristics of their individual patterns of settlement, place-name assignments, and attention to coastline detail. Also provided in these individualized map renditions are the major construction projects involving roads, airports, and other transportation facilities, which indicate the latest economic developments. Whenever possible, several portions of the new U.S.G.S. topographic maps of several of the selected islands have been photocopied and included.

Guam

Guam is a relatively large and high island situated on the Rimlands at the physiographic edge of the andesite line, at the southern end of the Mariana archipelago. (See Figure 35, page 86.) While the ratio of coastline to land area is high, as is true for

Photo 11. Limestone "bench," NE Guam

Figure 35. Mariana Islands

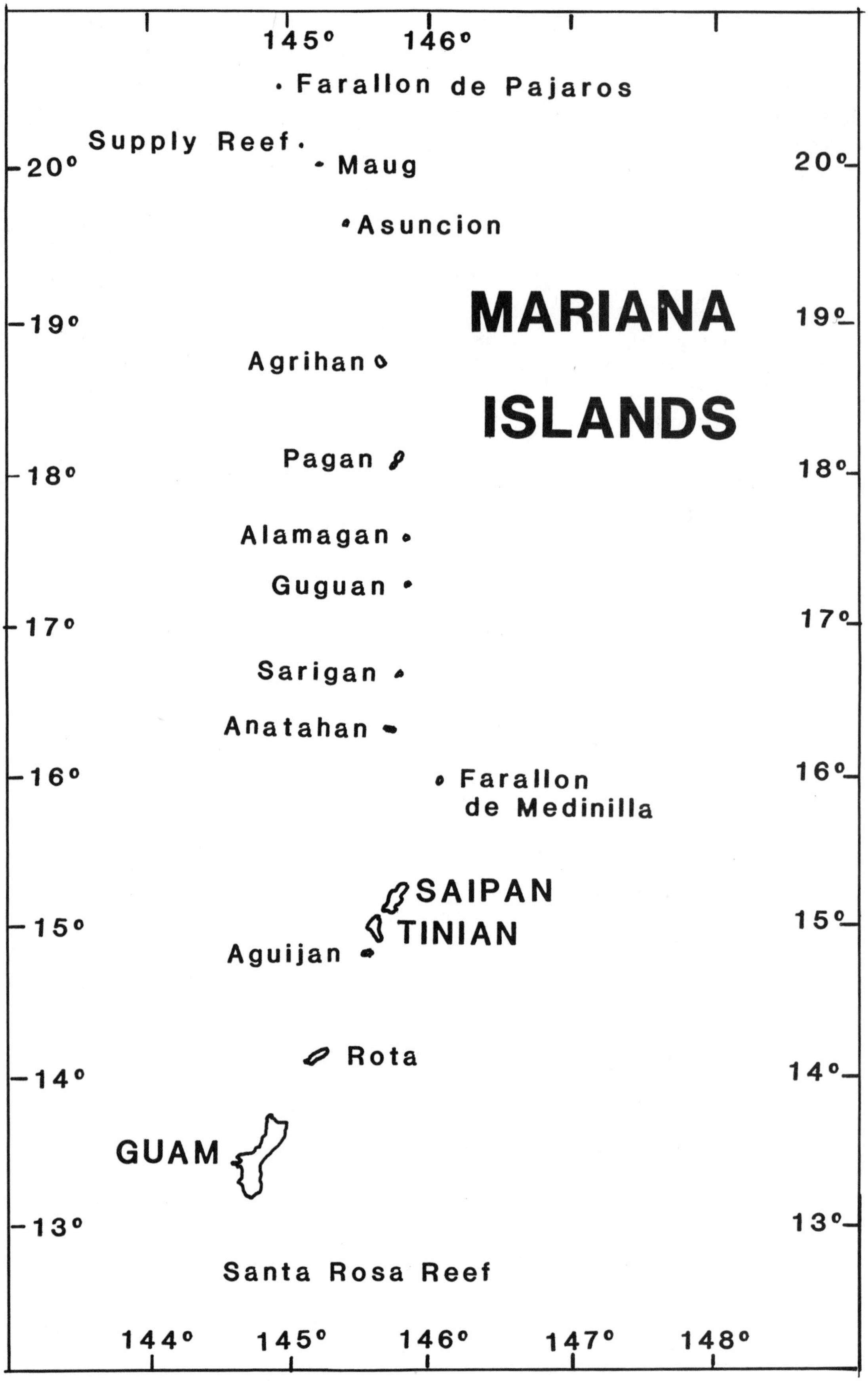

145°   146°

· Farallon de Pajaros

Supply Reef ·
—20°   · Maug   20°—

· Asuncion

MARIANA
—19°   19°—

Agrihan ◌

ISLANDS

Pagan ♪
—18°   18°—

Alamagan ·

Guguan ·
—17°   17°—

Sarigan ·

Anatahan ·
—16°   · Farallon   16°—
              de Medinilla

⌇SAIPAN
—15°   ⌇TINIAN   15°—
Aguijan ·

⌀ Rota
—14°   14°—

GUAM ⌀
—13°   13°—

Santa Rosa Reef

144°   145°   146°   147°   148°

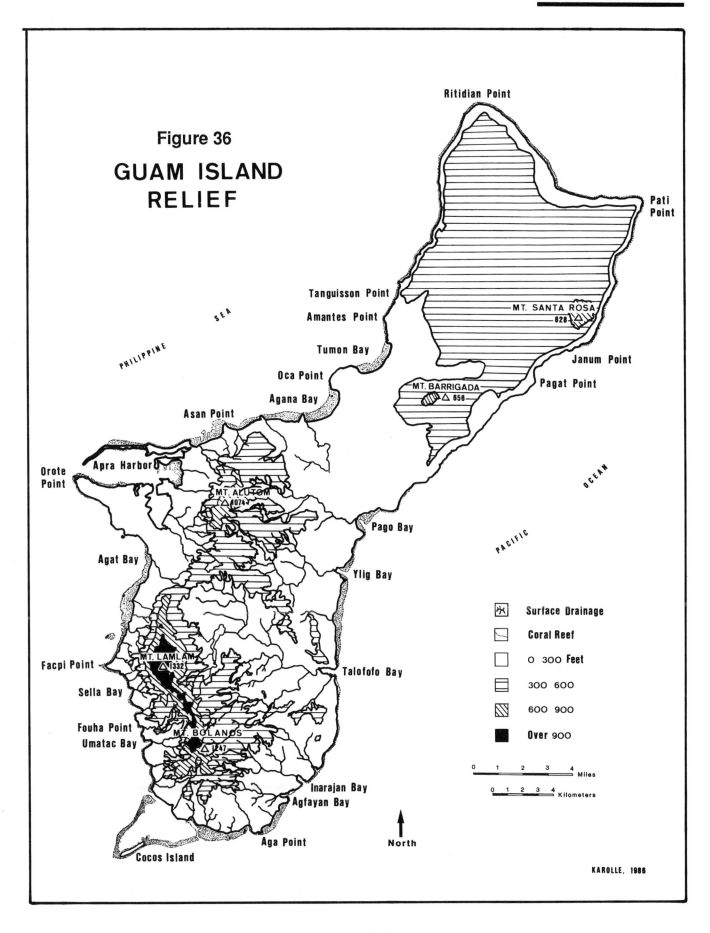

Figure 36

GUAM ISLAND
RELIEF

Ritidian Point

Pati Point

Tanguisson Point

Amantes Point

Tumon Bay

MT. SANTA ROSA
828

Oca Point

Janum Point

Agana Bay

MT. BARRIGADA
656

Pagat Point

Asan Point

PHILIPPINE SEA

Orote Point

Apra Harbor

MT. ALUTOM
1074

Pago Bay

Agat Bay

Ylig Bay

PACIFIC OCEAN

MT. LAMLAM
1332

Facpi Point

Sella Bay

Talofofo Bay

Fouha Point

MT. BOLANOS
1247

Umatac Bay

Inarajan Bay

Agfayan Bay

Aga Point

North

Cocos Island

Surface Drainage

Coral Reef

0 300 Feet

300 600

600 900

Over 900

0 1 2 3 4 Miles

0 1 2 3 4 Kilometers

KAROLLE, 1986

all islands in Micronesia, it is the geographic size and varied topography of Guam that explain much of its character. (See Figure 36, page 87.) One usually thinks of seascapes as dominating the vision of islanders, but the limited geographic size of Guam is in effect made larger by the uneven arrangement of the land surface. One can live and work for long periods of time on Guam and see very little of the ocean. This is due to the limited extent of the coastal plains, which are discontinuous and narrow along the periphery of the island. Consequently, although most of the population resides relatively close to these restricted lowlands, the people actually spend much of their time in the high areas.

Population Distribution

In 1986, the population of Guam was conservatively estimated to be 123,559 (and likewise, the 1990 Census reported 133,152), but these figures change continually with the movements of the military portion of the population. (See Figure 37, page 89.) Not only is w's population the largest of any single island in Micronesia, but the population density is also relatively high. The ratio of 577 people per square mile is comparable to that of many densely settled countries of Europe and Asia, such as the United Kingdom (598) and Sri Lanka (516). It is higher than that of the Philippines (351), but lower than that of Japan (758) and Taiwan (1,179).

The population density of the northern half of the island is nearly 800 people per square mile. Using as the central dividing line the Adelup Fault - which extends from Asan Village on the west coast through Agaña Heights across the narrow "waist" of the island and ends on the east side at Yona Village - 75 percent of the population lives in the northern half of Guam. The only densely settled areas in the southern half are the Naval Station and the adjacent villages of Agat and Safa Rita, both of which are south and east of Apra Harbor.

Cultural Diversity of the Population

The indigenous Chamorros remain the largest identifiable group. However, they constituted less than half of the population in 1984 (46 percent). During the historic Spanish period, the Chamorros made up at least 50 percent of the population, even during the period of population decline.

In 1984, the Filipino component of the population accounted for 21 percent and was larger than it had been at any time during the Spanish period. Mainland Americans, called "statesiders" or *haoles*, who replaced the ruling Spanish at the turn of the 20th century, now constitute nearly 19 percent. The remaining elements are mostly Asian and include relatively small numbers of Japanese, Chinese, Koreans, and Vietnamese. Recent migrations of Micronesians provide additional cultural diversity.

As the population expands, as it is doing so currently at an annual average rate of 2.5 to 2.9 percent, the need for conservation of the island's resources increases.

Geographic Divisions

For the purposes of geographical area studies, Guam is divided conveniently on a tri-regional basis: North, Central, and South Guam. (See Figure 38. page 91.) Three distinctive surface divisions are identified: the northern limestone plateau, the dissected volcanic plateau, and the coastal lowlands and associated fringing reefs. These divisions delineate well-established territorial zones reflecting topography and population designations.

The North region is the limestone plateau and represents an area of recent settlement. It was once dominated by low, tropical forests which were destroyed by wartime bombing and subsequent reconstruction. The villages and other built-up areas of Dededo, Yigo, Santa Rosa, and Mataguac (Agafo Gumas) are post-World War II settlements, while Tamuning and Tumon are older settlements accessible from Agaña and the Central regions.

The Central region topographically is an irregular area. Rocks are mixed; surfaces in the Barrigada, Mangilao, and Naval Air Station areas contrast with the steep dissection of the Agaña, Chaot, and Pago River areas of the Central region. The smoother limestone surfaces of Barrigada and Mangilao extend into the argillaceous limestone found in this transition zone between the North's flat reef-limestone plateau and the conglomerate and andesitic surfaces which extend into the South region. The main urban places of the Central region are Barrigada, Agaña Heights, Sinajana, Mongmong-Toto-Maite, Chalan Pago-Ordot, and Yona.

The South is largely a dissected volcanic upland with a low remnant edge of mountains paralleling the southwest coast. Narrow limestone

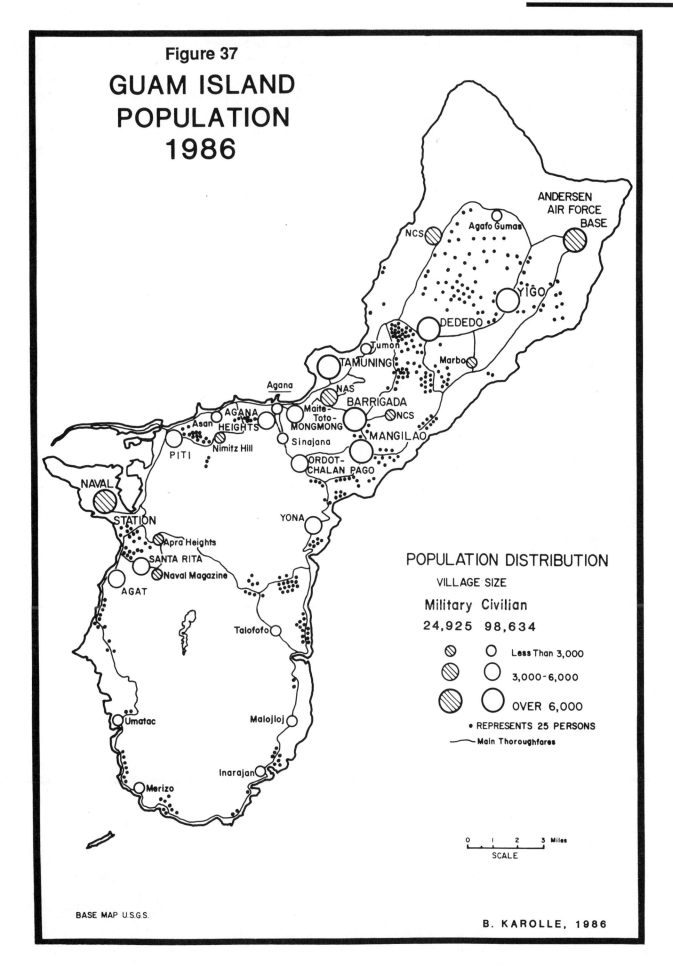

Figure 37

GUAM ISLAND POPULATION 1986

ANDERSEN AIR FORCE BASE

NCS
Agafo Gumas
YIGO
DEDEDO
Tumon
TAMUNING
Marbo
Agana
NAS
BARRIGADA
Maite-Toto-MONGMONG
Asan
AGANA HEIGHTS
NCS
Sinajana
MANGILAO
PITI
Nimitz Hill
ORDOT-CHALAN PAGO
NAVAL STATION
YONA
Apra Heights
SANTA RITA
Naval Magazine
AGAT
Talofofo
Umatac
Malojloj
Inarajan
Merizo

POPULATION DISTRIBUTION

VILLAGE SIZE

Military Civilian

24,925   98,634

Less Than 3,000

3,000-6,000

OVER 6,000

• REPRESENTS 25 PERSONS

— Main Thoroughfares

0   1   2   3 Miles

SCALE

BASE MAP U.S.G.S.

B. KAROLLE, 1986

deposits exist on the borders of the southeast coast. Most of the villages of the South are found along the coast, with the exceptions of Santa Rita and Talofofo. Westward around the periphery of the South region are the villages of Agat, Umatac, Merizo, and Inarajan.

Regional Node

Guam serves as a focal point of communication and transportation for American Micronesia. Several trans-Pacific communication cables exist to provide the region with international computerized telex and video services. These cables provide direct linkages to Southeast Asia and Japan, and across the Pacific to North America.

Apra Harbor, the island center for both large military and commercial shipping operations, is the largest and best-equipped harbor in the region. Additionally, the Guam International Airport provides regular daily and weekly air-cargo and passenger connections to most of the centers in Micronesia, Hawaii, and Southeast and East Asia.

Photo 12. Agaña, Guam, coastline and fringing reef

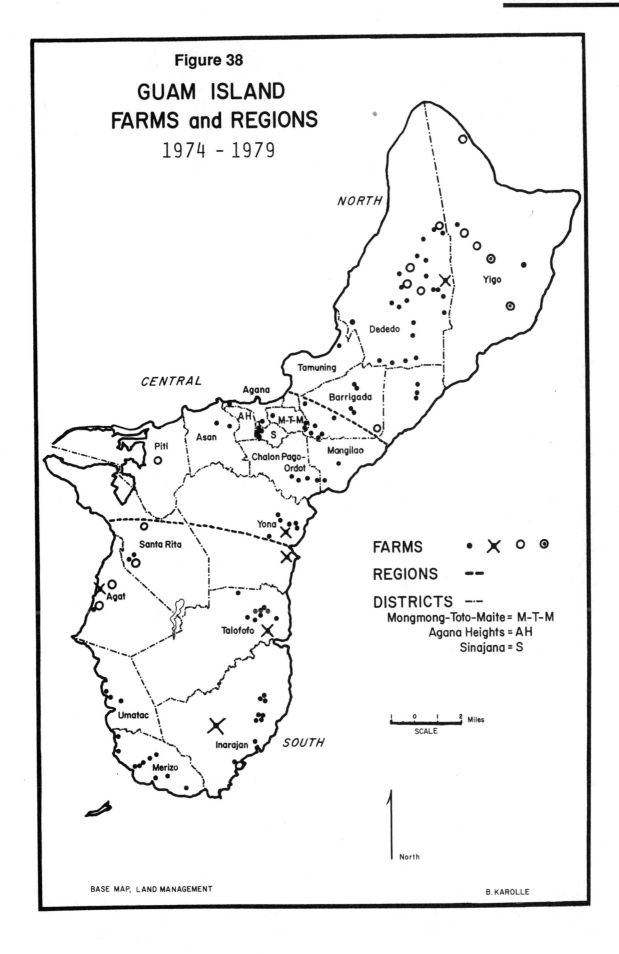

Figure 38

GUAM ISLAND
FARMS and REGIONS
1974 - 1979

NORTH

Yigo

Dededo

Tamuning

CENTRAL

Agana

AH

M-T-M

Asan

S

Pitl

Chalon Pago-Ordot

Barrigada

Mangilao

Yona

Santa Rita

Agat

Talofofo

Umatac

Inarajan

SOUTH

Merizo

FARMS • ✗ ○ ◉

REGIONS ‑‑

DISTRICTS ‑·‑
Mongmong-Toto-Maite = M-T-M
Agana Heights = AH
Sinajana = S

0   1   2 Miles
SCALE

North

BASE MAP, LAND MANAGEMENT

B. KAROLLE

Saipan

Saipan is a high island approximately forty-six square miles in area. (See Figure 39, page 93.) Irregularly shaped, the island is about thirteen miles long and five to six miles wide. The extensive limestone surfaces may be divided into three main regions: a coastal lowland including Tanapag Harbor in the west, where most of the 40,000 inhabitants live; a rugged northern and central upland constituting about two-thirds of the island (the northernmost area is called Makpe, or Marpi) and centrally located Mt. Takpochao at 1,529 feet; and the southern plateau including the Hakmang (Kagman) and Naftan peninsulas.

The northern interior is marked by surfaces of rising cliffs, terraces, and hilly terrain including a flattened ridge between 600 and 800 feet in elevation. The highest edge facing the east is known as Suicide Cliff; here a group of Japanese men, women, and children jumped to their deaths during the last days of the World War II invasion by the American armed forces. Nearby, on the extreme northern terraced coast, is another WWII landmark named Banzai Cliff.

Extending along the entire western side of Saipan is a relatively narrow coastal lowland. This area is fronted by a barrier reef of several miles in discontinuous length; it varies in distance from the shoreline from less than a quarter of a mile to one and a half miles offshore at its most distant point in Tanapag Lagoon and the Managaha Isle areas. In the wider southern portion of the coastal lowland is located the village of Susupi, and adjacent to the population center to the east is a marsh area called Susupi Lake.

Southeast of San Antonio village lies the plateau area, where new housing developments cover old Kobler Field, and the major site of the Saipan International Airport (previously, Isley Field). Both the Hakmang area to the northeast and the southern portions of Saipan remain relatively open and sparsely settled.

Saipan's habitation was severly reduced for more than a century after the Spanish removed the Chamorros in the late 17th century. The Spanish period dates from 1521 until 1899. Some migration and settlement from Guam and other islands occurred in the early 1800s. In 1810, the first small group of Carolinians (outer islanders from Yap and Truk), driven from their home islands by a typhoon, settled on Saipan. With the blessings of the Spanish, others followed to collect coconuts and dry the meat for copra. A few Chamorros came from Guam late in the Spanish period. The German census of 1902 recorded a local population of 1,631. The German administration lasted from 1899 until 1914, when the Japanese took over.

Saipan was the first island in the Mariana archipelago to be colonized and exploited by the Japanese. As did the Germans before them, they used Saipan as the administrative and commercial center of their Micronesian possessions. In 1939 Saipan had about 24,000 inhabitants, predominantly Japanese and Okinawans. Most of these inhabitants worked in commercial fishing and agricultural enterprises.

Sugarcane, grown for export, covered nearly 65 percent of the cultivated land (nearly 44,000 tilled acres in 1937), while subsistence crops such as tapioca, vegetables, sweet potatoes, papayas, bananas, and coffee accounted for most of the remaining 30 percent of Saipan's cropland. Sugar was milled at Chalan Kanoa, a town of 3,300 inhabitants on the southwest coast. Garapan, four miles to the north, was the main port and the largest town in the mandated Marianas. Its population of approximately 12,000 was engaged in administration, commerce, fishing, and the processing of fruits, vegetables, and marine products. Several villages served as local collection and distribution points for commercial farming and as minor government centers. Most of these settlements were destroyed during the American invasion of June and July 1944.

Saipan became the administrative center of the Trust Territory of the Pacific Islands (TTPI) on July 4, 1962. Between that time and mid-1979, the capital of the Trust Territory saw an influx of government personnel and resources. In 1975, when the covenant creating the Commonwealth of the Northern Mariana Islands (CNMI) was signed, the Trust Territory administration began the process of decentralization. Today, the nearly defunct Trust Territory headquarters at Capitol Hill houses several government agencies of Commonwealth.

Palau (Belau) Islands

The westernmost archipelagic component in the vast east-west Caroline Islands chain is known as Palau (Republic of Belau). (See Figure 40, page 94.) It consists of several physical formations and of twenty island units. The eminent scholar Edwin Bryan, Jr., in his 1971 *Guide*, listed 350 identifiable

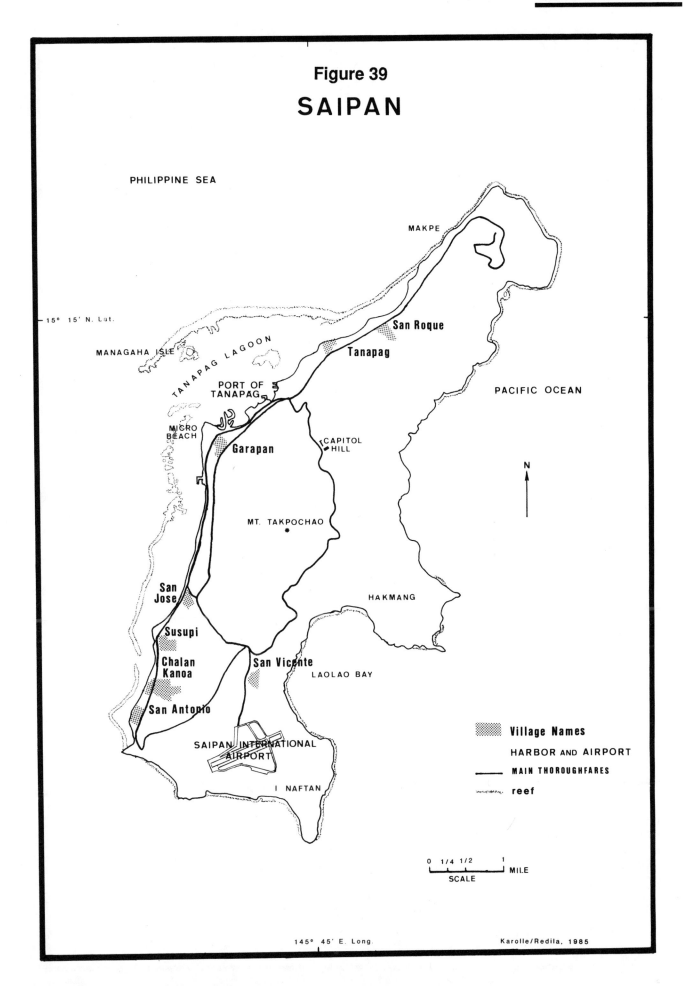

Figure 39

SAIPAN

PHILIPPINE SEA

MAKPE

15° 15' N. Lat.

MANAGAHA ISLE

TANAPAG LAGOON

San Roque

Tanapag

PORT OF
TANAPAG

PACIFIC OCEAN

MICRO
BEACH

Garapan

CAPITOL
HILL

N

MT. TAKPOCHAO

San
Jose

HAKMANG

Susupi

Chalan
Kanoa

San Vicente

LAOLAO BAY

San Antonio

SAIPAN INTERNATIONAL
AIRPORT

I NAFTAN

Village Names

HARBOR AND AIRPORT

MAIN THOROUGHFARES

reef

0 1/4 1/2 1
MILE
SCALE

145° 45' E. Long.

Karolle/Redila, 1985

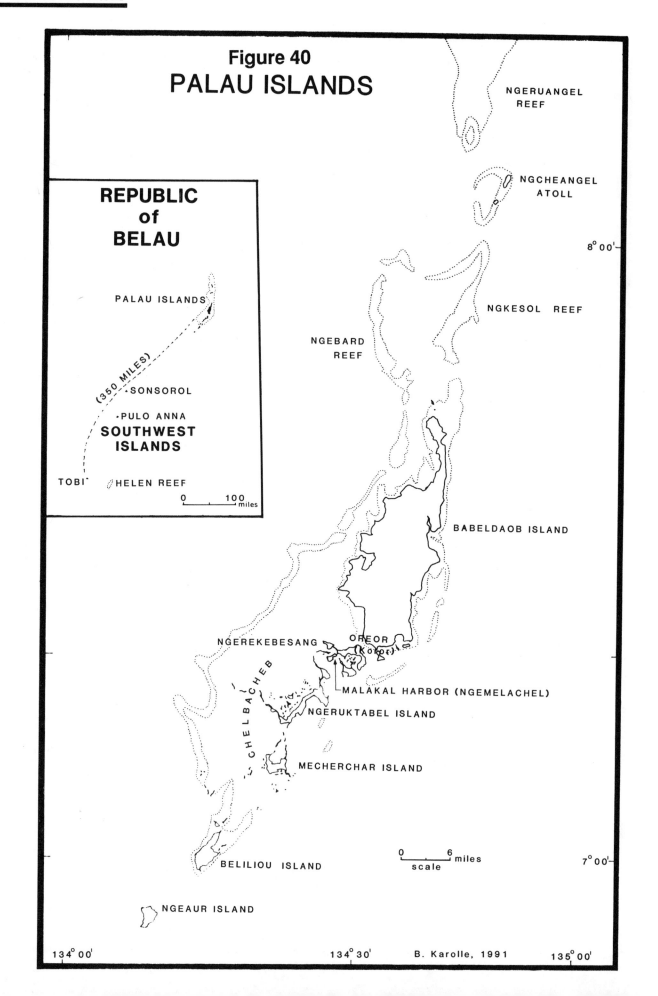

Figure 40
PALAU ISLANDS

NGERUANGEL REEF

NGCHEANGEL ATOLL

REPUBLIC of BELAU

PALAU ISLANDS

(350 MILES)

• SONSOROL

• PULO ANNA

SOUTHWEST ISLANDS

TOBI•   ⌐ HELEN REEF

0   100 miles

8° 00'

NGKESOL REEF

NGEBARD REEF

BABELDAOB ISLAND

NGEREKEBESANG

OREOR (Koror)

MALAKAL HARBOR (NGEMELACHEL)

NGERUKTABEL ISLAND

CHELBACHEB

MECHERCHAR ISLAND

0   6 miles
scale

7° 00'

BELILIOU ISLAND

NGEAUR ISLAND

134° 00'   134° 30'   B. Karolle, 1991   135° 00'

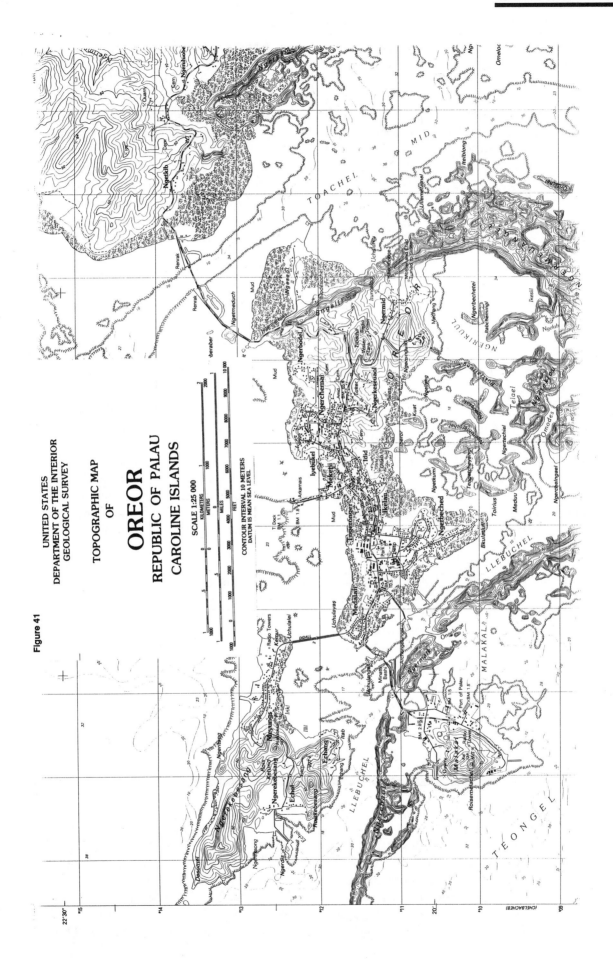

Figure 41

islands, atolls, islets, and reefs totaling 190.655 square miles of land. The enclosed area of lagoon is nearly 500 square miles.

The Palau archipelago is about 125 miles long and 25 miles wide. The capital, Oreor (Koror), is located on a small island of the same name. Oreor is located about 712 nautical miles southwest of Guam and 1,044 nautical miles east of Manila.

There are two major physical types of islands in Palau, volcanic and low coral (marine-limestone) islands. However, the Palaus also include several important variations and complex combinations. Babeldaob (Babelthuap) is volcanic; the relatively small but steep-sloped high "rock islands," called *Chelbacheb*, are limestone formations; Ngcheangel (Kayangel), north of Babeldaob Island, is an atoll; the small islands north of Beliliou (Peleliu) Island proper, situated on barrier reefs, are low platform reef islands or *motus*, (referred to here as islets); Ngeaur (Angaur) and Beliliou are relatively large raised limestone and volcanic formations.

Figure 31 shows the distribution of these main islands, the extensive barrier reef encircling much of the Palau group except Ngeaur, and the southwest outer islands. Additionally, the map reveals the relationships between the main landmass and the distant outer islands and atolls. For example, the outer island of Tobi, the westernmost inhabited island of the Republic of Belau, is located approximately 350 miles south-southwest of Oreor. Tobi is only 500 miles east of Mindanao Island in the southern Philippines, and about the same distance due north of the nearest land point of Irian Jaya (New Guinea), Indonesia.

The main islands - Babeldaob (Babelthuap), Oreor (Koror), Ngeruktabel (Urukthapel), Mecherchar (Eil Malk), and Beliliou (Peleliu) - are sur-rounded by a coral reef, about seventy miles long, that fringes the eastern shores and widens out on the western side. On the western side of the islands, the lagoon is about forty miles long and eight miles wide. The reef is difficult to cross, except in a few places, even for the Palauan canoes. To the north of the main islands is an atoll (two by five miles) with four low, sandy islets: the Ngcheangel (Kayangel) islands, rising a few feet above water. Slightly to the south of the main islands is a raised atoll, Ngeaur (Angaur), which at one time contained important phosphate deposits. All mining activities occurring in Ngeaur ceased when the U.S. Navy closed operations in 1952.

Babeldaob, the largest island of the Palau group, is pear-shaped, widest toward the southern end, and narrows to a slender peninsula in the north. It is about twenty-three miles long and varies in width from four to eight miles. The total area of Babeldaob is approximately 141 square miles. The island has several lines of hills with a maximum elevation of 700 feet. Babeldaob is composed of volcanic rock, except for some raised coral formations in the south. The coastal lowlands are covered with mangrove forest, while most of the hilly interior is wooded or savanna vegetation.

The population of Palau has fluctuated from an estimated 3,750 in 1900 to a high of 22,077 in 1938. This latter figure, however, included only 6,377 indigenous Palauans; the remainder were Japanese, concentrated in Oreor. The Japanese left Babeldaob to the Palauans and sent only a few administrators and some mining personnel to the island.

The total population of the Palau Islands in 1946 was 6,500, most of whom lived on Babeldaob in villages along the coast. Irrai (Airai), the largest village during the Japanese period, located in southern Babeldaob (near the present international airport), had a population of about 700.

In 1984, the total population of Palau was approximately 13,000, with 7,585 residing in Oreor. With the construction of several bridges and access roads, Oreor now is conveniently linked to the adjacent islands of Babeldaob, Ngemelachel (Malakal), and Ngerekebesang (Arakabesan). (See Figure 41, page 95.)

The Yap Islands

Yap consists of four main islands: Yap, Gagil Tamil, Maap, and Rumung, plus about ten very small islands. These tightly clustered islands are parts of a single triangularly shaped submarine platform and are surrounded by a fringing reef. (See Figure 42, page 97.) The reef varies in width from one-half to two miles. The islands enclosed by it make a compact group sixteen miles long and eight miles wide. The total land area is approximately thirty-nine square miles. The reefs enclose about ten square miles of lagoon.

The Yap Islands are the top of a great submarine ridge similar in formation to the island arcs of Palau and the Marianas. They rise from the eastern edge of the Philippine plate and follow the andesite line north toward Japan. The eastern side

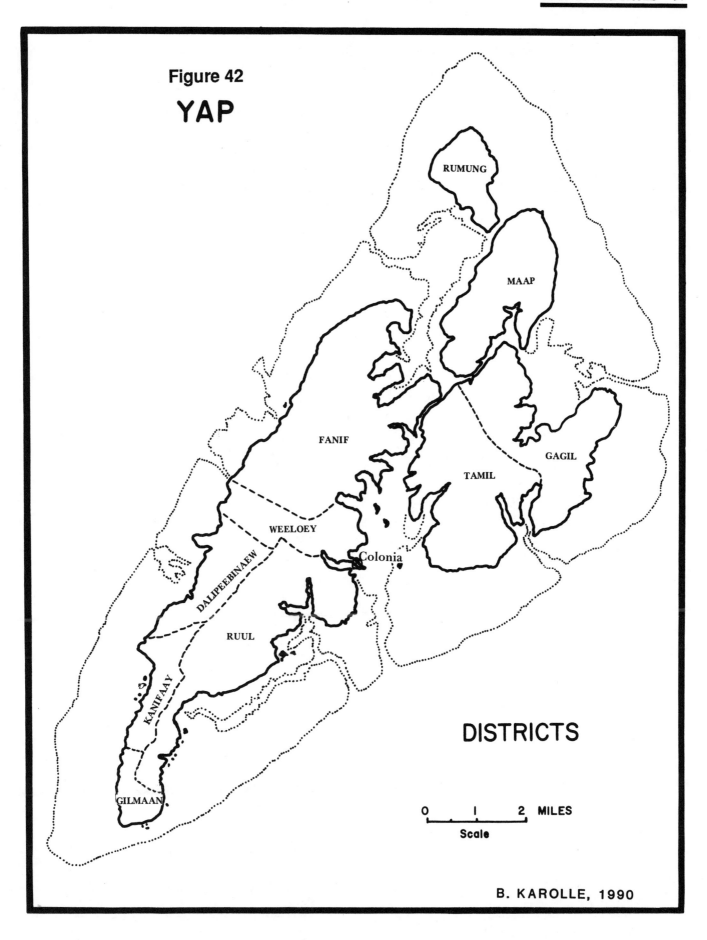

Figure 42

YAP

RUMUNG

MAAP

FANIF

GAGIL

TAMIL

WEELOEY

Colonia

DALIPEEBINAEW

RUUL

KANIFAAY

GILMAAN

DISTRICTS

0   1   2 MILES
Scale

B. KAROLLE, 1990

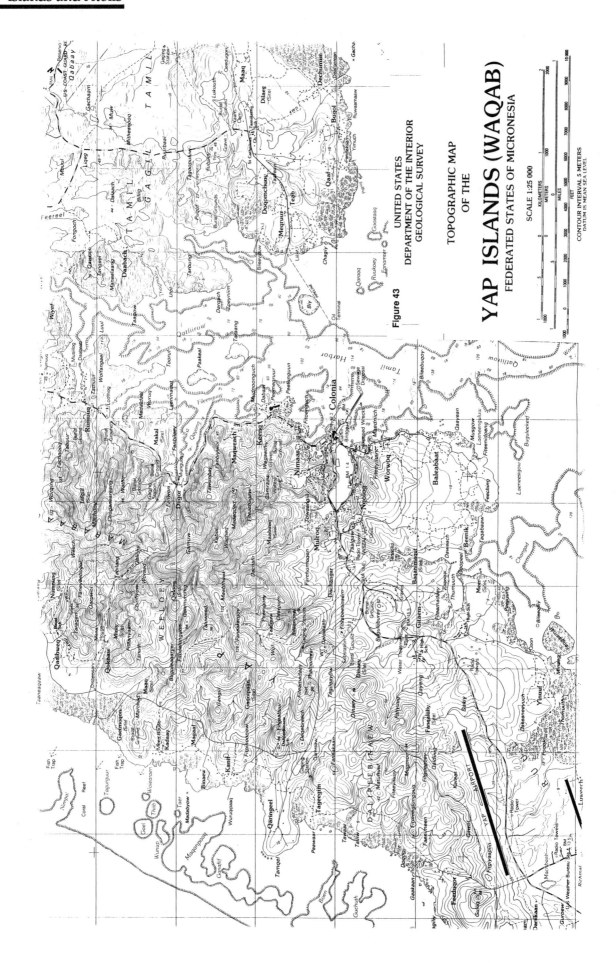

Figure 43

UNITED STATES
DEPARTMENT OF THE INTERIOR
GEOLOGICAL SURVEY

TOPOGRAPHIC MAP
OF THE

YAP ISLANDS (WAQAB)
FEDERATED STATES OF MICRONESIA

SCALE 1:25 000

CONTOUR INTERVAL 5 METERS
DATUM IS MEAN SEA LEVEL

of Yap is marked by a deep subduction trench in the ocean floor. While the core of the island group is of metamorphic rock, the eastern portion is composed of weathered volcanic materials. The most marked erosion of this ridge and the greatest elevation occur on the eastern side.

Also, regional subsidence has produced sea flooding in the erosional valleys. With heavy rainfall and a high runoff rate, coral growth has been retarded and the resulting estuaries have formed natural channels in the reef. Yap and Gagil Tamil were nearly separated, except for a narrow neck of land, by the subsidence that formed Tamil Harbor. The Germans completed the geologic separation by digging the Tagireeng Canal. Figures 42 and 43, pages 97 and 98, show these narrow channels extending north to south from Tamil Harbor to the narrows between Fanif and Gagil Tamil districts.

Tamil Harbor, one of the largest of these "drowned" estuaries, is the main commercial harbor. It is located on the southeastern side of Yap. Although it is the best harbor in the Yap Islands, it has a narrow and dangerous entrance. The coral-free channel is about one hundred yards wide at its narrowest point near the entrance from the Pacific Ocean.

About two miles north-northwest of the Tamil Harbor entrance is the capital of Colonia with a population of nearly 2,500. The town site is situated on the largest of the individual islands, Yap itself, which is about twelve miles long and one to three miles wide. The highest elevation of the whole group, less than 600 feet above sea level, is near the northern end of Yap. From these northern hills the land slopes downward toward both sides of the island. Most of the southeastern portion of Yap is low, with mangrove forests. Mangrove forests are also found, but discontinuously, on the western and northern coastlines of Yap.

Chuuk (Truk)

The Chuuk Islands are located some 650 nautical miles southeast of Guam and about 1,400 nautical miles north of Port Moresby in Papua New Guinea.

Photo 13. Chuuk Lagoon "high island" seascape

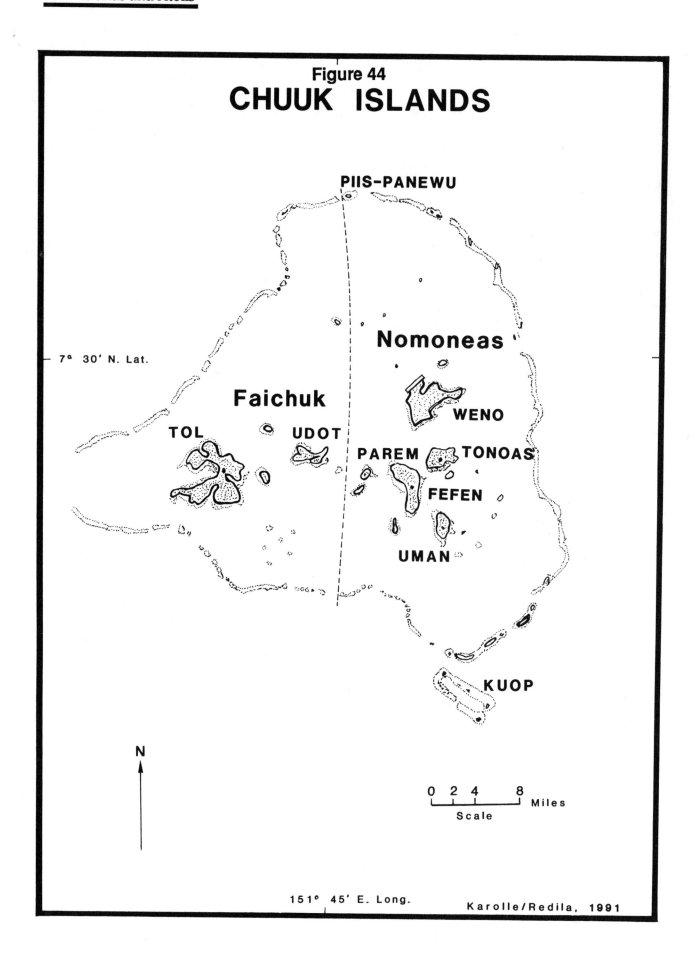

Figure 44
CHUUK ISLANDS

7° 30' N. Lat.

151° 45' E. Long.

Karolle/Redila, 1991

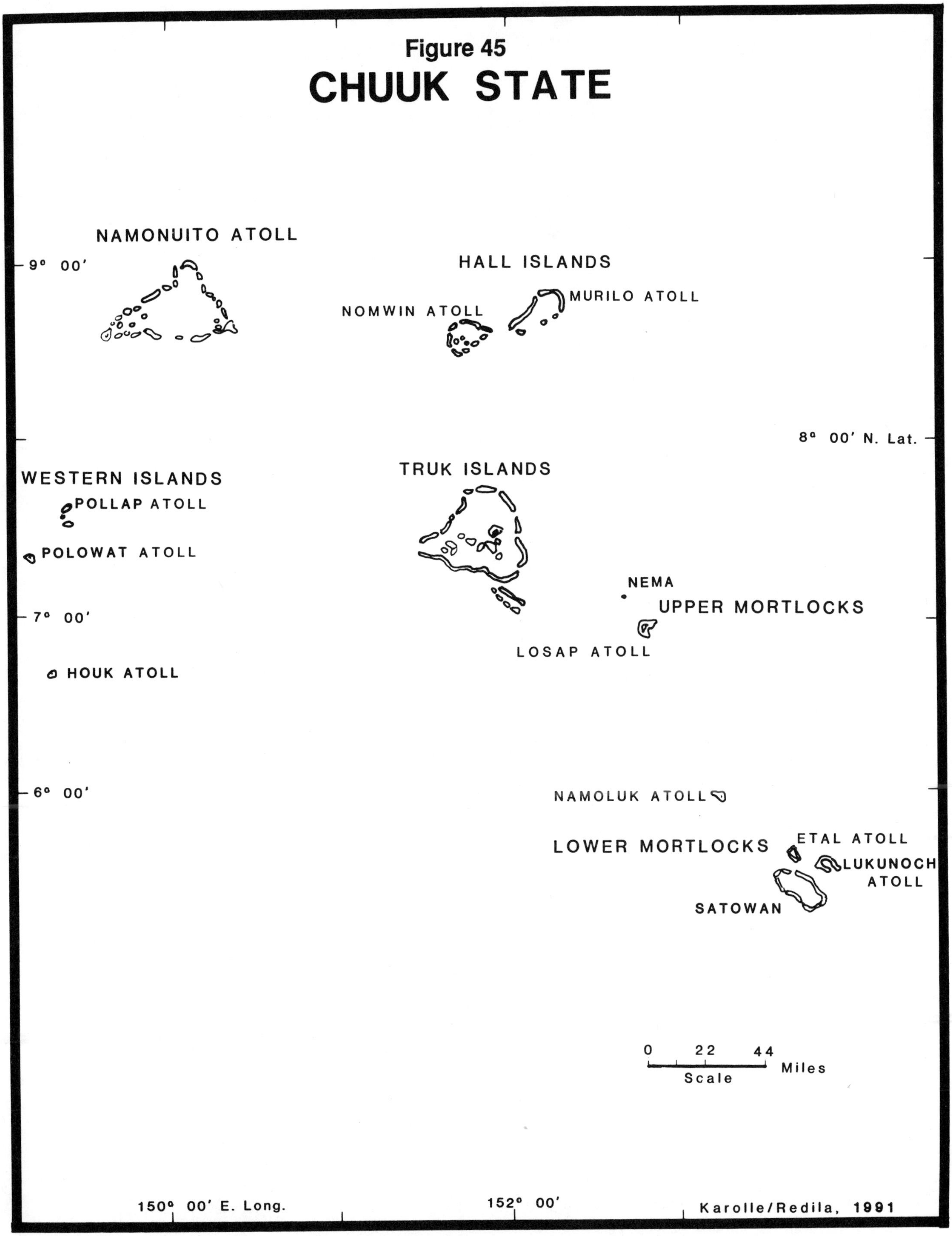

Figure 45

CHUUK STATE

NAMONUITO ATOLL

— 9° 00'

HALL ISLANDS

NOMWIN ATOLL   MURILO ATOLL

8° 00' N. Lat.

WESTERN ISLANDS

POLLAP ATOLL

POLOWAT ATOLL

TRUK ISLANDS

NEMA

UPPER MORTLOCKS

— 7° 00'

LOSAP ATOLL

HOUK ATOLL

— 6° 00'

NAMOLUK ATOLL

LOWER MORTLOCKS   ETAL ATOLL

LUKUNOCH
ATOLL

SATOWAN

0   22   44
|____|____| Miles
Scale

150° 00' E. Long.   152° 00'   Karolle/Redila, 1991

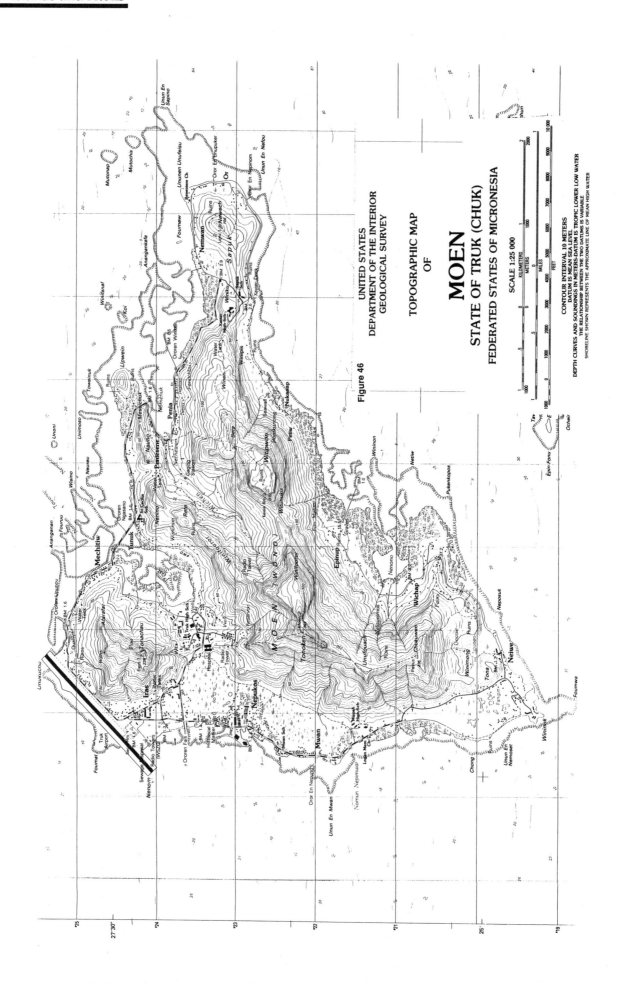

UNITED STATES
DEPARTMENT OF THE INTERIOR
GEOLOGICAL SURVEY

TOPOGRAPHIC MAP
OF

MOEN
STATE OF TRUK (CHUK)
FEDERATED STATES OF MICRONESIA

SCALE 1:25 000

CONTOUR INTERVAL 10 METERS
DATUM IS MEAN SEA LEVEL
DEPTH CURVES AND SOUNDINGS IN METERS-DATUM IS TROPIC LOWER LOW WATER
THE RELATIONSHIP BETWEEN THE TWO DATUMS IS VARIABLE
SHORELINE SHOWN REPRESENTS THE APPROXIMATE LINE OF MEAN HIGH WATER

Figure 46

The group is close to the geographic center of the State of Chuuk, in the Federated States of Micronesia, near the coordinates of 7.30 degrees north latitude, 151.45 degrees east longitude. (See Figures 44 and 45, page 100 and 101.)

Chuuk is a complex group with a barrier reef that varies from thirty to forty-five miles in diameter. There are about sixty-nine small islets on the barrier reef, only one of which, Piis-Panewu, on the north side, is permanently inhabited. Chuuk Lagoon is large and extremely deep; in some areas the depth of the lagoon is over 200 feet. The lagoon's circumference is approximately 140 miles, and it contains seven large high islands and many smaller ones. The total land area of the island group is approximately thirty-four square miles. Tol includes Pata in the NW, Wonei in the NE, and Polle in the SW, and is the largest of the islands. Tol's Mt. Winipot, at 1,463 feet, is the highest point in the Chuuk group. Other important islands in order of size are Weno, the state capital, Fefen, Tonoas (Dublon), Udot, Uman, and Parem. The highest elevations on these islands range from about 800 feet to more than 1,000 feet.

The Chuuk Islands are of volcanic origin. The complex is composed of the deeply eroded summit of a former volcanic dome that rises from a submarine plateau. Although the islands of the eastern part of the plateau, such as Moen, appear to be fairly stable, there has been some recent subsidence in the western areas of Chuuk as is evidenced by drowned river valleys.

A traditional east-west division exists in the Chuuk complex between the Faichuk island group in the west and the Nomoneas island group in the east, which has developed economically more rapidly in recent times. Tonoas (Dublon) used to be the center of the Japanese administration and had a Japanese town that was entirely destroyed during World War II. Under the American administration, Weno (Moen) became the district center. (See Figure 46, page 102.) Port facilities and a modern airport were constructed in the 1970s. The town has a population of about 13,800. Several hotels form the core of a modest tourism industry.

Pohnpei (Ponape)

Pohnpei is a volcanic dome similar in origin to Truk but much less advanced in subsidence. Nearly oval in shape, the island is approximately fourteen miles from north to south and sixteen miles from east to west. It is surrounded by some forty small islands of both coral and volcanic origin. (See Figure 47, page 104.) The whole island formation is encircled by a barrier reef that encloses a relatively narrow lagoon. The lagoon and surrounding reef area cover about eighty square miles. The total dry-land area has been estimated at 130 square miles, which makes Pohnpei the third largest island in Micronesia, after Guam with 214 square miles, and Babeldaob, in Palau, with 141 square miles. Pohnpei and the nearby atolls of Ant and Pakin are also known as the Senyavin Islands.

Pohnpei consists of several ranges of sharply eroded peaks separated by deep valleys which radiate from the center of the island. In the center is a peak of 2,533 feet, Mt. Nanlaud, which makes Pohnpei the second highest island in Micronesia, after Agrihan, in the northern Marianas, which has an elevation of 3,165 feet. Faulting has produced steep cliffs in the columnar basalt. The Sokehs island cliff rises some 900 feet above sea level. It is located to the north of Pohnpei proper and is visible from Kolonia, the main town. The principal areas of level land are distributed along the coasts and on faulted surfaces near the shores, especially in the north. (See Figure 48, page 105.)

In recent times, the northern coastal areas around Kolonia and the adjacent municipalities of Sokehs, Net, and Uh have experienced the greatest development and population growth. However, with the completion of the around-the-island perimeter road, which connects all the districts including the municipality of Madolenihmw in the southeast part of Pohnpei, many more areas are accessible today. For instance, the ancient ruins of Nan Madol (Madolenihmw) are the most historic site; as early as the 1180s, Nan Madol was the center of Pohnpei. A leading educational center, the Ponape Agriculture and Trade School (Pats), is located near Nan Madol.

Under the Japanese administration, the town of Kolonia had approximately 8,000 inhabitants (today's population is nearly 6,000). Most of the Japanese were engaged in local industries producing food and goods for export. Agricultural development was boosted with the establishment of the Tropical Industries Research Institute in 1926. The Japanese not only made Pohnpei self-supporting in food but also developed a significant export trade in copra, ivory, nuts, starch (tapioca), dried bonito fish, and bauxite. The fertile coastal

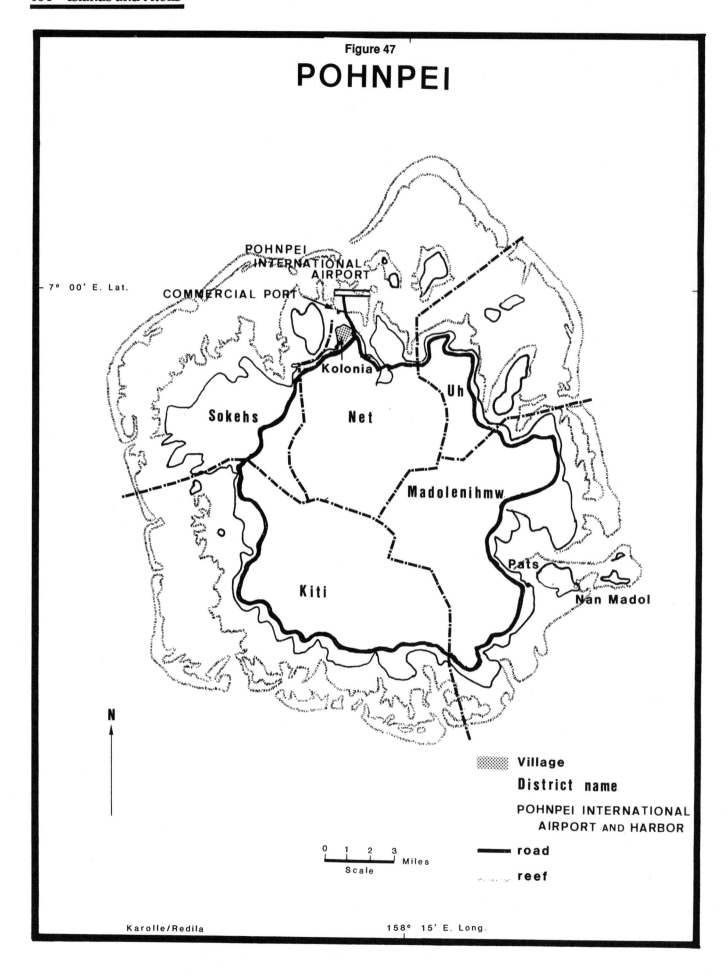

Figure 47

POHNPEI

POHNPEI
INTERNATIONAL
AIRPORT

COMMERCIAL PORT

− 7° 00′ E. Lat.

Kolonia

Uh

Sokehs

Net

Madolenihmw

Kiti

Pats

Nan Madol

N

Village

District name

POHNPEI INTERNATIONAL
AIRPORT AND HARBOR

road

reef

0   1   2   3
Miles
Scale

Karolle/Redila

158° 15′ E. Long.

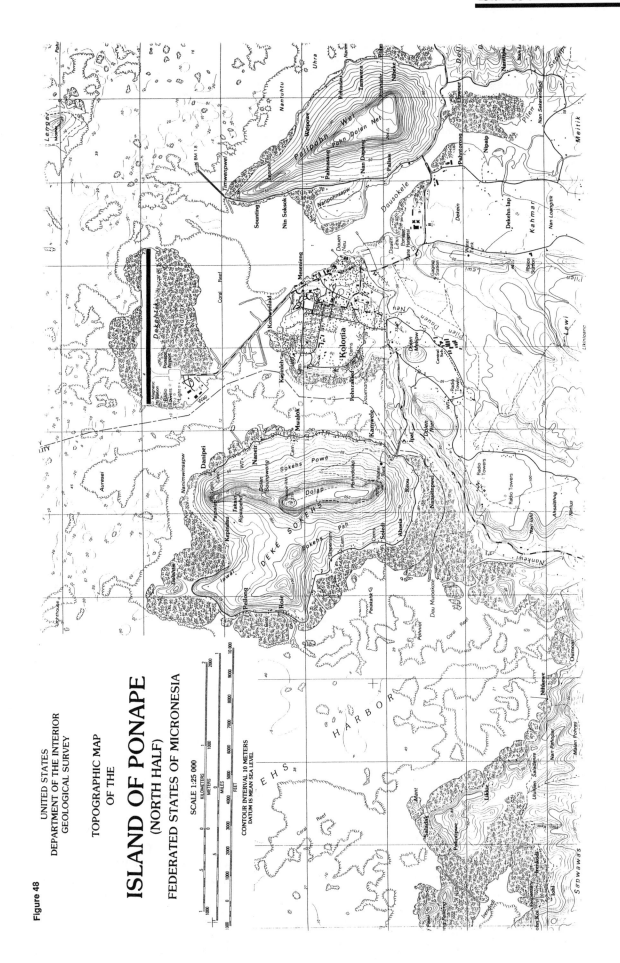

Figure 48

UNITED STATES
DEPARTMENT OF THE INTERIOR
GEOLOGICAL SURVEY

TOPOGRAPHIC MAP
OF THE

ISLAND OF PONAPE
(NORTH HALF)

FEDERATED STATES OF MICRONESIA

SCALE 1:25 000

CONTOUR INTERVAL 10 METERS
DATUM IS MEAN SEA LEVEL

plains and plateaus made Pohnpei one of the most productive islands for commercial agriculture during the Japanese period.

From 1947 onward, political education overshadowed economic development. The following chronology gives some idea of the direction in which Pohnpei district developed: in 1966 the first U.S. Peace Corps volunteers arrived, to eventually number as many as 120. In 1970, the Community College of Micronesia was established, and the first fourteen-member American Civic Action Team arrived to work on construction projects. In 1972, future political status negotiations began and culminated on May 10, 1979, in Pohnpei's official incorporation into the Federated States of Micronesia.

Kosrae

Kosrae is a high island located at 5.30 degrees north latitude and 163.00 degrees east longitude. It is the easternmost of the Caroline Islands and the easternmost state in the Federated States of Micronesia. The island measures roughly eight and one-half by ten miles, with an area of approximately forty-two square miles. (See Figure 49, page 107.)

Most of Kosrae is made up of two rugged basaltic mountain masses with sharp ridges and deeply eroded valleys characteristic of young mountain landscapes. A high valley divides the mountainous interior into two sections. The southern range forms a compact mass in the center of the island with numerous peaks. Mt. Finkol (Crozer), at 2,077 feet, is the highest. Both mountain masses are bordered by an alluvial coastal plain of varying width, usually not in excess of one mile.

The coastal plains are densely covered with either mangrove or coconut palms. The mangroves flourish along the reef areas and shoreline and are so dense that landing is difficult. Inland from the mangroves, there is a belt of coconut, mango, and breadfruit trees. This is where the Kosraeans live. Most of the primary forests that used to cover the mountains of the interior have been destroyed and replaced by secondary forests - consisting of trees thirty to forty feet high - which when mixed with shrubs are also virtually impenetrable.

Kosrae is divided into four districts, each of which has at least one village and several scattered hamlets. In 1984 the island's population was 6,262. The district of Lelu borders the harbor and the small island of the same name where Kosrae's largest and most important village, Lelu, is located. Lelu's population in 1984 was estimated at somewhat more than 2,500.

In the near future, an all-weather road will connect Lelu and Tafunsak. This road will provide easy access to the new Kosrae International Airport in the northern coastal area of Okat. There is also a small airstrip near Lelu Village.

The entire north and northeast coasts are in the district of Tafunsak. Tafunsak Village is about four miles from Lelu Village by the old coastal road, which is periodically covered with coral rubble and sand.

The old mission station at Insiaf (Woot) is on the northwest side of the island. It is accessible from the village of Tafunsak by canoe via a route within the reef and may be reached from Utwe at high tide via a canal through the mangrove swamps.

The district of Malem is just south of Lelu along the southern portion of the east coast. Malem Village is about three miles from Lelu Harbor via the perimeter road.

The district of Utwe comprises the southern portion of Kosrae. Utwe Village lies on a low spit of land which is almost completely covered by the year's highest tides. The road which passes through Malem ends at Utwe Village, a distance of about four miles.

Majuro Atoll (Ratak Chain)

Majuro is an atoll located in the southeastern area of the Marshall Islands. (See Figures 1, 12, and 50, pages 2, 28, and 108.) The chain or group of atolls begins in the north at Bokaak and extends to Mili in the south. Majuro serves as the capital of the Republic of the Marshall Islands.

The capital is located on Dalap Islet, a district which is found on the east side of Majuro near the Port at Uliga. Both the Nitijela (house of parliament) and the executive building are found on this part of the atoll.

Majuro, with a land area of less than four square miles, had a population in 1984 of 12,747 and has two major population centers: Laura Village, at the western end, and the newer urbanized area on the eastern side. Majuro Atoll surrounds a lagoon of more than 113 square miles, which is a typical atoll size for the Marshalls. There are a dozen larger atolls in the group.

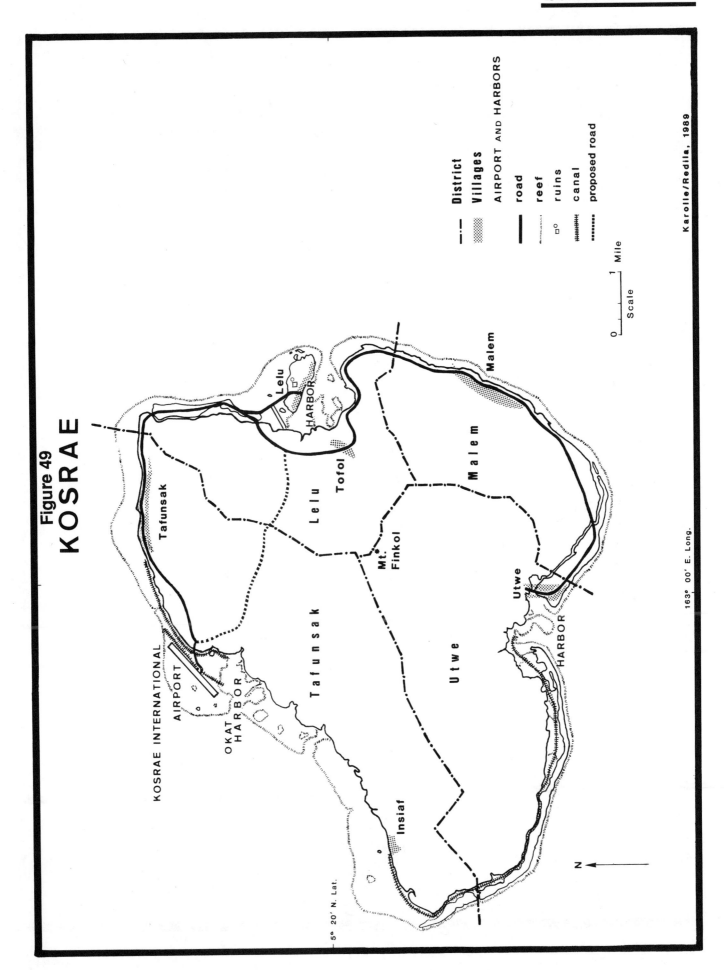

Figure 49
KOSRAE

District
Villages
AIRPORT AND HARBORS
road
reef
ruins
canal
proposed road

0   1 Mile
Scale

Karolle/Redila, 1989

163° 00' E. Long.

5° 20' N. Lat.

Tafunsak

Lelu

Tofol

Malem

Malem

Lelu

HARBOR

Mt. Finkol

Utwe

Utwe

HARBOR

KOSRAE INTERNATIONAL AIRPORT

OKAT HARBOR

Tafunsak

Insiaf

N

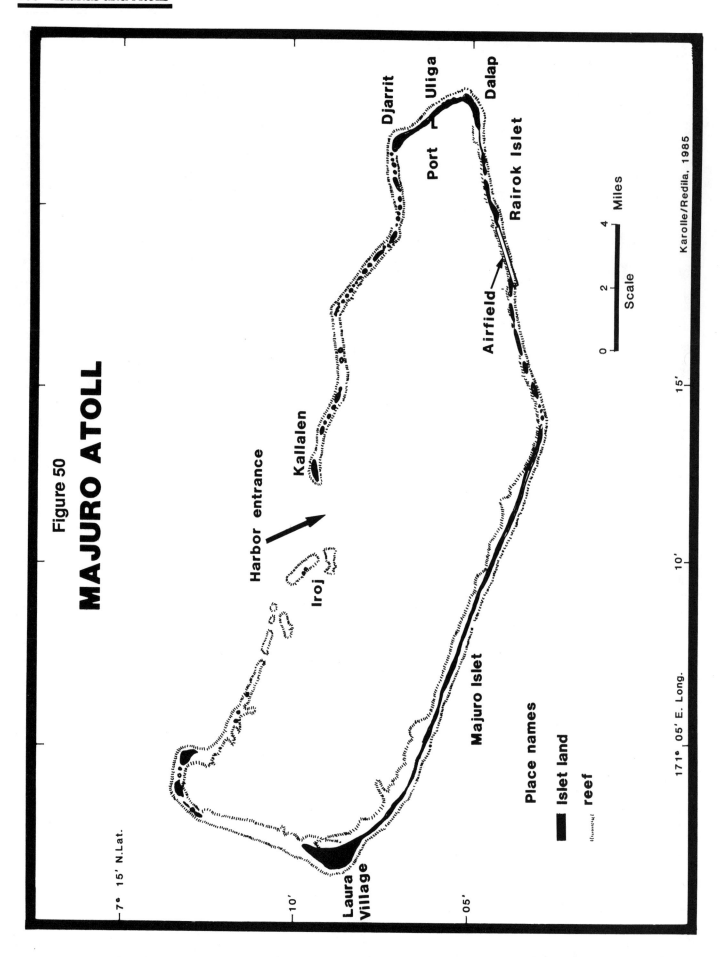

Figure 50

MAJURO ATOLL

Place names

Islet land

reef

Karolle/Redila, 1985

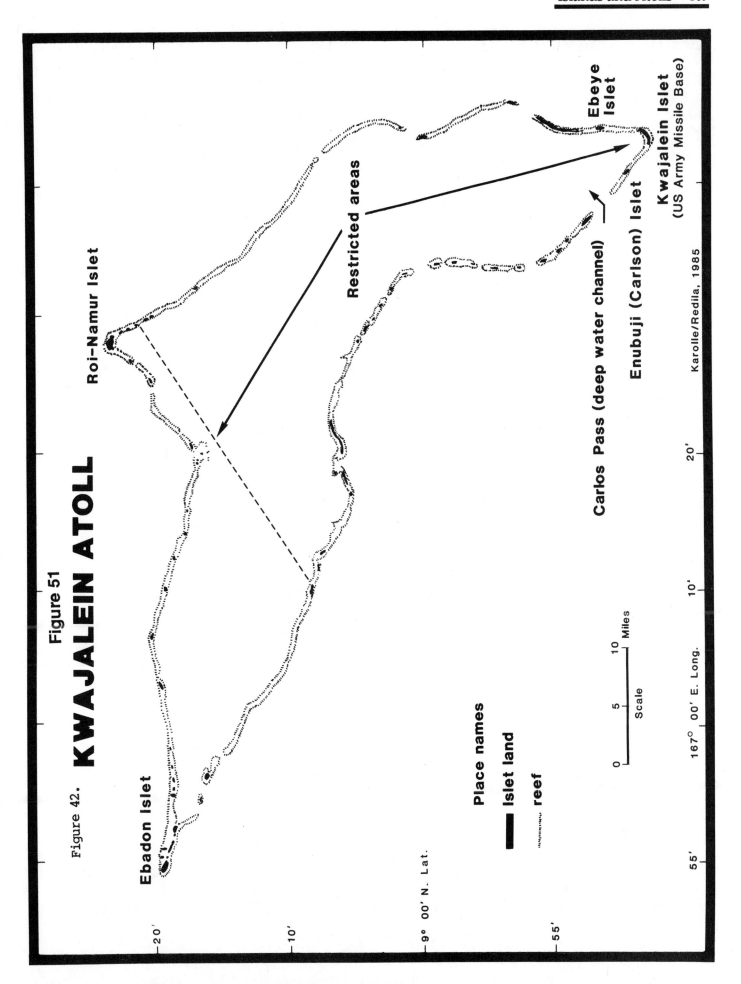

Figure 51

Figure 42. **KWAJALEIN ATOLL**

Ebadon Islet

Roi-Namur Islet

Restricted areas

Ebeye Islet

Kwajalein Islet
(US Army Missile Base)

Carlos Pass (deep water channel)

Enubuji (Carlson) Islet

Karolle/Redila, 1985

Place names
Islet land
reef

Scale

0   5   10 Miles

167° 00' E. Long.

9° 00' N. Lat.

20'

10'

55'

20'

10'

55'

Kwajalein Atoll (Ralik Chain)

Kwajalein (see Figures 1, 12, and 51, pages 2, 28, and 109) is the world's largest atoll formation, with slightly more than five and one-half square miles of land distributed around a lagoon of some 138 square miles. The lagoon follows a curving line beginning at Ebadon Islet in the northwest to Kwajalein Islet in the southeast, a distance of ninety miles. The distance across the lagoon from Roi-Namur in the north directly to the south is twenty miles.

Although Majuro is the administrative center, Kwajalein is the main center of employment. The U.S. Department of Defense's Army Missile Base is located on Kwajalein Islet and occupies most of the land and lagoon. It is from this base that the MX and other intercontinental ballistic missiles are coordinated by radar-monitoring installations with other military facilities in California. It is estimated that $1 billion has already been invested in the base, which has an annual budget of some $170 million. Thousands of Marshallese are employed at or depend on this complex for their livelihood. Most local employees live on Ebeye Islet, four miles away, and commute daily by boat to the base.

Photo 14. Tropical sky and trees

UNITS OF MEASUREMENT AND CONVERSIONS

Reporting Grid/Map Positions

Geographic coordinates of latitude and longitude are reported in degrees and minutes of arc distance based upon the following relationship: 1 degree of latitude/longitude = 60 minutes of arc distance (1 minute of arc distance = 60 seconds). For example: the parallel of latitude 13 degrees and 31 minutes north is written in the text as 13.31 degrees north latitude, while on the map figures the same would appear as 13° 31' N. Lat., or north latitude.

Note: 1 degree of latitude = 60 nautical miles; 1 minute of latitude = 1 nautical mile.

A. Length (distance)

    1. 1 statute mile = 5,280 feet = 1.6093 kilometers
    2. 1 nautical mile = 6,076 feet = 1.8531 kilometers

    Conversions:

        1. nautical miles times 1.151 = statute miles
        2. nautical miles times 1.8531 = kilometers

B. Area

    1. 1 square mile = 2.5899 square kilometers

    Conversions:

        Square miles times 2.5899 = square kilometers

C. Velocity

    1. 1 knot (kt.) = 1.151 miles per hour

    Conversions:

        Knots times 1.151 = statute miles per hour

BIBLIOGRAPHY

A Micronesian Voice. 1989. Issue #75, January 27, Honolulu: FSM Citizens Association of Hawaii.

Alkire, William H. 1977. *An Introduction to the Peoples and Cultures of Micronesia.* Menlo Park: Cummings.

_____. 1965. *Lamotrek Atoll and Inter-Island Socioeconomic Ties.* Illinois Studies in Anthropology, No. 5. Urbana: University of Illinois Press.

Amerson, A. Jr. 1969. *Ornithology of the Marshall and Gilbert Islands.* Atoll Research Bulletin 127:1-348.

Ashby, Gene. 1983. *A Guide to Ponape: An Island Argosy.* Eugene, Oregon: Rainy Day.

Barraclough, Geoffrey, ed. 1984. *The Times Atlas of World History.* Maplewood, NJ: Hammond.

Bellwood, Peter. 1980. *The Peopling of the Pacific. Scientific American,* 243(5): 174-185.

_____. 1979. *Man's Conquest of the Pacific.* New York: Oxford.

Best, Bruce, et al. 1990. *The University of Guam's Experience in Delivering Distance Education.* Educational and Training Technology International, 27(3): 257-263.

Bowers, Neal M. 1951. *The Mariana, Volcano, and Bonin Islands.* In Otis W. Freeman, ed. *Geography of the Pacific,* pp. 205-235.

_____. 1950. *Problems of Resettlement on Saipan, Tinian and Rota, Mariana Islands.* Ph.D. dissertation, University of Michigan. Ann Arbor: University Microfilms.

Bryan, Edwin H., Jr. 1971. *Guide to Place Names in the Trust Territory of the Pacific Islands.* Honolulu: Bishop Museum.

Buck, Peter H. 1953. *Explorers of the Pacific: European and American Discoveries in Polynesia.* Special Pub. 43, Honolulu: Bishop Museum.

Chisholm, Michael. 1982. *Modern World Development: A Geographical Perspective.* Totowa, NJ: Barnes and Noble.

Cohen, Benjamin J. 1973. *The Question of Imperialism: the Political Economy of Dominance and Dependence.* New York: Basic Books.

Council of Biology Editors. 1972. *Style Manual.* Third edition, Washington D. C.: American Institute of Biological Sciences.

Craig, Robert D. and Frank P. King, eds. 1981. *Historical Dictionary of Oceania.* Westport, CT: Greenwood.

Cumberland, Kenneth B. 1968. *Southwest Pacific: A Geography of Australia, New Zealand, and Their Neighbors.* New York: Praeger.

Dahlgren E.W. 1916. *Were the Hawaiian Isands Visited by the Spaniards Before Their Discovery by Captain Cook in 1778?* 57:4, Stockholm: Almovist & Wilksells Boktryckeri-A.-B.

Decker, Robert and Barbara Decker. 1981. *Volcanoes.* San Francisco: Freeman.

Dickenson, J. P., et al. 1983. *A Geography of the Third World.* New York: Methuen.

Driver, Marjorie ., transl. 1989. *Fray Juan Pobre in the Marianas 1602.* Mangilao, Guam: Micronesian Area Research Center, University of Guam.

_____. 1987. *Navigational Data for the Mariana Islands.* Mangilao, Guam: Micronesian Area Research Center, University of Guam.

_____. 1985. *Guam: A Nomenclatural Chronology.* Educational Series No. 5, Mangilao, Guam: Micronesian Area Research Center, University of Guam.

_____ . 1983. *Fray Juan Pobre de Zamora and His Account of the Mariana Islands. Journal of Pacific History,* 18 (3-4):198-216. Canberra: Australia University.

Economic Research Center. 1990. *1989 Guam Annual Economic Review and Statistical Abstract, 1976, 1975, 1981, 1982, 1985 and 1987.* Department of Commerce, Government of Guam, Agaña: Guam.

Fages, Jean and Fr. T. B. McGrath. 1975. "Tourism Development in Guam and Tahiti: A Comparison," in *The Impact of Urban Centers in the Pacific.* Roland Force and Brenda Bishop, editors. Honolulu: Pacific Science Association.

Fosberg, F. Raymond. 1960. *The Vegetation of Micronesia*. Bulletin American Museum of Natural History, 119(1): 1-75.

_____. 1953. *Vegetation of Central Pacific Atolls: A Brief Summary*. Atoll Research Bulletin, 23:1-26.

Fosberg, F. R. and M-H. Sachet. 1975. *Flora of Micronesia, 1: Gymnospermae*. Smithsonian Contributions to Botany, 20: 1-15.

Fosberg, F. R., M.-H. Sachet and R. Oliver. 1987. *A Geographical Checklist of the Micronesian Monocotyledonae. Micronesica*, 20(1-2): 19-129.

_____. 1987. *A Geographical Checklist of the Micronesian Pteridophyta and Gymnospermae. Micronesica*, 18(1): 23-82.

_____. 1979. *A Geographical Checklist of the Micronesian Dicotyledonae. Micronesica*, 15(1-2): 41-295.

Freeman, Otis W., ed. 1951. *Geography of the Pacific*. New York: Wiley.

Friis, Herman R. ed. 1967. *The Pacific Basin: A History of Its Geographical Exploration*. Special Pub. No. 38. New York: American Geographical Society.

Furtado, C. 1964. *Development and Underdevelopment*. Berkeley: University of California Press.

Gale, Roger W. 1977. *Micronesia: A Case Study of American Foreign Policy*. Ph.D. dissertation, Department of Political Science, University of California, Berkeley.

Gladwin, Thomas. 1970. *East Is a Big Bird: Navigation and Logic on Puluwat Atoll*. Cambridge, MA: Harvard University Press.

Glassman, Sidney F. 1952. *The Flora of Ponape*. B. P. Bishop Museum Bulletin, 209: 1-152.

Guam Visitors Bureau. 1987-1991. Annual and Monthly Reports, to July 1991. Tamuning: Guam.

Hezel, Francis X., S.J. 1983. *The First Taint of Civilization: A History of the Caroline and Marshall Islands in Pre-Colonial Days, 1521-1885*. Honolulu: University of Hawaii Press.

High Commissioner. 1981-1982. Annual Reports. Trust Territory of the Pacific Islands, U.S. Department of Interior, Washington, D.C.: U.S. Government Printing Office.

Howells, William. 1973. *The Pacific Islanders*. New York: Scribner.

Karolle, Bruce G. 1988. *Atlas of Micronesia*. Guam Publications, Inc., Agaña: Guam.

_____. 1985. (Guam) "Typhoons." Panorama, *The Guam Tribune*, 3(19): 2-4, Agaña: Guam.

_____. 1984. "Economic Development in Micronesia," "Island Views," *Glimpses*, p. 63-64, Agaña: Guam.

_____. 1983. (Guam) "Earthquakes." Panorama, *The Guam Tribune*, Agaña: Guam, 2(41): 4-5.

_____. 1982. "Pacific Rimlands: A Geographic Focus on Micronesia." Panorama, *The Guam Tribune*, 1(10): 3-4. Agaña: Guam.

_____. 1981. "Micronesia: A Geographical Definition." In Robert D. Craig and Frank P. King, eds. *Historical Dictionary of Oceania*, Westport, CT: Greenwood, pp. 186-187.

_____. 1978. *Agriculture, Population, and Development in Guam Island: Some Options for the Future*. Ph.D. dissertation, Department of Geography, Michigan State University.

_____. 1976. "A Geography of Micronesian Copra." *Guam Recorder*, 16(1): 37-49. Agaña: University of Guam.

Karolle, Bruce G. and Dirk A. Ballendorf. 1986. *Prospects for Economic Self-Sufficiency in the New Micronesian States*. Centre for Southeast Asian Studies, Occasional Paper No. 25. Australia: James Cook University.

Karolle, Bruce G. and Dave Antonelli. 1985. *Geographical Knowledge in American Micronesia*. Bulletin of the Illinois Geographical Society, 28(2): 28-34. Normal: Illinois State University.

Karolle, Bruce G. and Donald C. Jones. 1977. *Territoriality: A Basic for Determining the Future of Micronesia. Pacific Asian Studies*, 2(1 & 2): 32-41.

Kent, Noel J. 1983. *Hawaii: Islands Under the Influence*. New York: Monthly Review Press.

Lessa, William A. 1950. "Ulithi and the Outer Native World." *American Anthropologist*, 52: 27-52.

Lewis, David. 1972. *We, the Navigators: The Ancient Art of Landfinding in the Pacific*. Honolulu: University Press of Hawaii.

Mandy, J. F. *Climatological Data for Guam, Mariana Islands*. U.S. Naval Oceanography Command Center, Joint Typhoon Warning Center, Tech. Note 85-1. Guam.

Marsh, William M. and Jeff Dozier. 1981. *Landscape: An Introduction to Physical Geography*. Menlo Park, CA: Addison-Wesley.

Mathieson, Alister and Geoffrey Wall. 1982. *Tourism: Economic, Physical and Social Impacts*. New York: Longman.

Maxwell, Bruce D. 1982. *Floristic Description of Native Upland Forests on Kosrae, Eastern Caroline Islands*. *Micronesica*, 18(2): 109-120.

Mayer, Peter C. 1975. *The Visitor Industry on Guam: The Social-Economic Impact of Modern Technology Upon a Developing Insular Region: Guam, Vol. II*. Agaña: University of Guam.

Monmaney, Terence. 1990. "Annals of Science: This Obscure Malady." *The New Yorker*, 29 October.

Montvel-Cohen, Marvin. 1970. *Canoes in Micronesia*. Micronesian working papers, No. 2., Agaña: University of Guam.

Morgan, William N. 1988. *Prehistoric Architecture in Micronesia*. Austin: University of Texas Press.

Motteler, Lee S. 1986. *Pacific Island Names: A Map and Name Guide to the New Pacific*. Honolulu, HI: Bishop Museum Press.

Murphy, Raymond E. 1980. "American Micronesia: A Supplementary Chapter in the Regional Geography of the United States," *Journal of Geography*, 79(5): 181-186.

_____. 1950. *The Economic Geography of a Micronesian Atoll, Mokil*. Annals. Washington: Association of American Geographers, 40(1): 53-83.

_____. 1949. "High and Low Islands in the Eastern Carolines," *Geographical Review*. New York: American Geographical Society, 39(1): 425-439.

_____. 1948. "Landownership on a Micronesian Atoll, Mokil." *Geographical Review*. New York: American Geographical Society, 38(4): 598-614.

Myrdal, Gunnar. 1963. *Economic Theory and Underdeveloped Regions*. London: Methuen.

Navy Department. 1948. *Handbook on the Trust Territory of the Pacific Islands*. Appendix D., Trusteeship agreement. Washington, D.C.

New Zealand Meteorological Service. 1984. *Climate Data of Gilbert Group*. Ministry of Transport. Wellington: New Zealand.

Office of Planning and Statistics. 1986. *First National Development Plan, 1985-1989*. Federated States of Micronesia, Kolonia: Pohnpei, FSM.

Office of Planning and Statistics. 1985. *Abstract of Statistics, 1984*. Koror: Republic of Palau.

Oliver, John E. 1979. *Physical Geography: Principles and Applications*. North Scituate, Mass.: Duxbury Press.

Pacific Islands Yearbook. 1984. Sydney: Pacific Publications.

Pomeroy, Earl S. 1951. *Pacific Outpost: American Strategy in Guam and Micronesia*. Stanford: Stanford University Press.

Pray, Martin. 1976. *Growth and Effect of Air Charters on Guam's Tourist Industry*. Pacific Asian Studies Association, 1(2): 9-10. Agaña: University of Guam.

Price, Willard. 1966. *America's Paradise Lost*. New York: Day.

Rajotte, Freda and Ron Crocombe, editors. 1980. *Pacific Tourism as Islanders See It*. South Pacific Social Sciences Association and the Institute of Pacific Studies: Fiji.

Rostow, Walter W. 1960. *The Stages of Economic Growth*. Cambridge: Cambridge University Press.

Sadler, James C. 1969. *Average Cloudiness in the Tropics from Satellite Observations*. Honolulu: East-West Center Press.

Safford, William E. 1905. *The Useful Plants of the Island of Guam*. Contributions for the United States National Herbarium, Smithsonian Institution, 9: 1-416.

Shirley, Rodney W. 1983. *The Mapping of the World*. London: Holland Press.

Shutler, Richard, Jr., and Mary E. Shutler. 1975. *Oceanic Prehistory*. Menlo Park: Cummings.

South Pacific Commission. 1983. *Overseas Trade 1981*. Statistical Bulletin of the South Pacific 23. Noumea: New Caledonia.

Spate, O. (Oskar) H. K. 1988. *The Pacific Since Magellan, Volume III: Paradise Found and Lost*. Minneapolis: University of Minnesota Press.

_____. 1983. *Volume II: Monopolists and Freebooters*. Minneapolis: University of Minnesota Press.

_____. 1979. *Volume I: The Spanish Lake*. Canberra, Australia: Australian National University.

Stanford Research Institute. 1974. *A Study and Review of Laws Pertaining to Alien Investment on Guam, Vol. I*. Menlo Park: California.

_____. 1986. *Economic Benefits from Tourism to Guam*. Final Report. Menlo Park: California.

Stone, Benjamin C. 1970. *The Flora of Guam. Micronesica*, 6: 1-659.

Tajima, Yasuhiro. 1986. "Development of the Tourist Industry in Federated States of Micronesia from the Viewpoint of Economic Independence," pp. 85-91, in the *Prompt Report of the Fourth Scientific Survey of the South Pacific*. Research Center for the South Pacific, Kagoshima University, Japan, and the Community College of Micronesia, Kolonia: Pohnpei: FSM.

Tarawa Teacher's College. 1976. *These Are the Gilberts*. Curriculum Development Unit. Tarawa: Kiribati.

Taylor, Ronald C. 1973. *An Atlas of Pacific Islands Rainfall*. Institute of Geophysics, Data Report, 25. Hawaii: University of Hawaii.

Thomas, Stephen D. 1987. *The Last Navigator*. Henry Holt: New York.

Thomas, William L., Jr. 1967. "The Pacific Basin: An Introduction." In Herman R. Friis, ed. *The Pacific Basin: A History of Its Geographical Exploration*. New York: American Geographical Society.

U.S. Department of Commerce, Environmental Science Services Adm., 1969. *Climates of the World*. Washington, D. C.: Environmental Data Service.

U.S. Department of the Interior, Geological Survey. 1983. *Topographic Maps*. Menlo Park, CA: National Mapping Division.

U.S. Department of State. 1984. *Annual Report on the Administration of the Trust Territory of the Pacific Islands*. Washington, D.C.

U.S. National Oceanic and Atmospheric Administration (U.S. NOAA). 1984a. *Local Climatological Data, Annual Summary: Guam, Pacific; Honolulu, Hawaii; Johnston Island, Pacific; Kwajalein; Marshall Islands, Pacific; Majuro, Marshall Islands, Pacific; Pago Pago, American Samoa; Ponape Island, Pacific; Truk, Eastern Caroline Is., Pacific; Wake Island, Pacific; Yap Island, Pacific*.

_____. 1984b. *Climatological Data, Annual Summary, Hawaii and Pacific*.

U.S. Naval Oceanography Command Center. 1984. Joint Typhoon Warning Center, Annual Tropical Cyclone Report. Guam.

Vail, Carl J. 1975. *The Economy, The Social-Economic Impact of Modern Technology upon a Developing Insular Region: Guam, Vol. II*. Agaña: University of Guam.

Van der Brug, Otto. 1985. *Compilation of Water Resources Development and Hydrologic Data of Saipan, Mariana Islands*. U.S. Geological Survey, Water-Resources Investigations Report. 84-4121.

_____. 1984a. *The 1983 Drought in the Western Pacific*. U.S. Geological Survey, W.R.I.R. 85-418.

_____. 1984b. *Water Resources of Kosrae, Caroline Islands*. U.S. Geological Survey, W.R.I.R. 83-4161.

_____. 1984c. *Water Resources of the Palau Islands*. U.S. Geological Survey, W.R.I.R. 83-4140.

_____. 1984d. *Water Resources of Ponape, Caroline Islands*. U.S. Geological Survey, W.R.I.R. 83-4139.

_____. 1983a. *Water Resources of the Truk Islands*. U.S. Geological Survey, W.R.I.R. 82-4082.

_____. 1983b. *Water Resources of Yap Islands*. U.S. Geological Survey, W.R.I.R. 82-357.

Vaugondy, Robert. 1764. *Les Isles*. Ayala Museum, "East Indies" 11 x 14. Manila, Philippines.

Warner, Don C., 1978. *A Decade of Tourism: The Socio-Economic Impact of Guam's Visitor Industry*. Guam Visitors Bureau, Agaña: Guam.

Warner, Don. C., James A. Marsh and Bruce G. Karolle. 1979. *The Potential for Tourism and Resort Development in Palau: A Socio-Economic-Ecological Impact Study*. Agaña: University of Guam.

Wiens, Herold J. 1962. *Pacific Island Bastions of the United States*. Searchlight Series 4. Princeton: Van Nostrand.

Wilson, W. Scott. 1968. *Land and Social Organization of Lelu, Kosrae*. Ph.D. dissertation, Department of Anthropology, University of Pennsylvania

Wyrtki, Klaus and G. Meyers. 1975. *The Trade Wind Field Over the Pacific Ocean. Part I. The Mean Field and the Mean Annual Variation, H.I.G.-75-1. Part II. Bimonthly Fields of Wind Stress, H.I.G.-75-2*. Institute of Geophysics, Hawaii: University of Hawaii.

INDEX

120